KERI LEHMANN

Subatomic Faith

Birthing Heaven to Earth Through the Quantum Realm

First published by 100X Publishing 2023

Copyright © 2023 by Keri Lehmann

All rights reserved. No part of this publication may be reproduced, stored or transmitted in any form or by any means, electronic, mechanical, photocopying, recording, scanning, or otherwise without written permission from the publisher. It is illegal to copy this book, post it to a website, or distribute it by any other means without permission.

Keri Lehmann asserts the moral right to be identified as the author of this work.

Keri Lehmann has no responsibility for the persistence or accuracy of URLs for external or third-party Internet Websites referred to in this publication and does not guarantee that any content on such Websites is, or will remain, accurate or appropriate.

Designations used by companies to distinguish their products are often claimed as trademarks. All brand names and product names used in this book and on its cover are trade names, service marks, trademarks and registered trademarks of their respective owners. The publishers and the book are not associated with any product or vendor mentioned in this book. None of the companies referenced within the book have endorsed the book.

Unless otherwise noted, all Scripture quotations are taken from the Holman Christian Standard Bible®, Copyright © 1999, 2000, 2002, 2003, 2009 by Holman Bible Publishers. Used by permission. Holman Christian Standard Bible®, Holman CSB®, and HCSB® are federally registered trademarks of Holman Bible Publishers.

First edition

ISBN: 978-1-7339893-8-1

Illustration by Andrea Calvery

This book was professionally typeset on Reedsy.
Find out more at reedsy.com

Dedicated to my favorite, Aaron Lehmann:
I love my life with you, on Earth, in Heaven, and in all our dreams:
in every imaginable possibility.

To my momma, Donna Wilson:
Your blood courses through my veins.
I'm the fruit of your choices- You took from the Tree of Life:
That life flows through me; Many benefit from it.

for Melissa

We take the land!

♡, Ca...

Hear the ice crack across the lake.
Water drips off leaves wrapped in snow.
And on the ground below
is green.
Come alive.
Come alive.
Dreams.
Green.

-"Green" Aaron Lehmann, 2018

Contents

Foreword		ii
Preface		v
Acknowledgement		xv
Introduction: God Said Write. NOW.		xvii
1	The Dream	1
2	Historical Set-Up	6
3	The Interpretation	9
4	The TRUE Mother Births Life into Freedom	20
5	The Slave Woman Births Life into Slavery	25
6	The Three Realms	30
7	The Good News of the Gospel of Peace	54
8	Don't Be Drunk and Half-Asleep	66
9	The Violent Take It by Force	81
10	Faith or Faint- You Can't Do Both	95
11	Mediator. Media. Medium. Mayhem.	107
12	Fight To Kill or Fight To Win	127
13	A Time for Everything Under Heaven	141
14	CIA Got Nothing on The Kingdom	150
15	REST	156
16	Sabbath Flow™	168
Afterword		178
About the Artist		183
About the Author		186

Foreword

I was hesitant to write a book on this subject for several reasons.

1. I am neither a physicist nor a neuroscientist.
2. I am also not a theologian or preacher.
3. I don't debate with strangers.
4. I still feel like I am sorting this subject out for myself.
5. I take my role as a resource of information very seriously and always want to share truth only.

But one day in November 2022, as you will see in the introduction, the Lord told me to write. He also told me to shut down every "media" that I usually listen to (all my YouTube teachers and those who have influence in my mind), and only read or listen to the Bible. So I did, for two months. I listened to scriptures all day as I worked, and all night as I slept; meanwhile, I wrote almost daily.

As I wrote, it felt like I wasn't saying much of anything- the words flowed out, but they seemed insignificant. But each time that I would go back to see where I was at, I was met with surprise and awe of God's ability to speak through me concerning His power in us, despite all of my weaknesses.

Much of what you are about to read has been formulated in my mind over the past decade through expansive research and real-world application. I always test what I learn: I'm an entrepreneur. We make thoughts come to life.

The newest concept for me in this book is the matter of matter: quantum science. I've been studying this topic loosely since 2015, and more vigorously since 2019. Everything else has been a lifelong education.

They say that it takes 10,000 hours to become an expert at something. While I don't have a degree in science or theology (I have an associate's degree in art and science, and a cosmetology license since 1994), I have more than fulfilled the required hours of study for general knowledge. Anyone who knows me knows my voracity for researching the Bible, science, the natural world, the spirit realm, the human mind, and especially regarding the subject matter at hand: real-life application in humans for successful living. I eat, sleep, and literally dream it. I have for decades. I never stop.

And while I am grateful to God for the ability to read, decipher, categorize, and distill information from scientific journals, books, videos, and articles, I would like to say in full disclosure:

If a physicist wants to debate me on my assertions of quantum mechanics in this book, it isn't going to go well for me. Haha! I understand the science enough to write this book, and a little bit more every day. As I dig into the study of quantum mechanics, I've found that even among the scientists, there isn't complete harmony of fact, and they debate one another, along with armchair physicists, in search of truth. It's all any of us want. It's a noble work. As such, I feel qualified to throw my hat into the ring, playing to my strengths of Biblical knowledge, understanding of the spiritual realms, wisdom of the inner working of the human mind, and the ability to read between the lines of creation. I'm extremely intuitive.

Everything I've stated within the book, I firmly believe to be factual according to what I currently know and have experienced. But as I always say, "Facts change. Truth never changes." For this reason, I always use the Bible (the Truth) as the foundation of what I build in my mind and hands, and then I look to science (facts) to harmonize with the Word of God. And it does and is, increasingly so, as God has allowed more revelation to us all. That's why I'm writing this book: Scientific research and the Word of God are excitingly coming together rapidly before our eyes, and more obviously to those who have attuned spiritual eyes to see. But know: any scientific knowledge requested of me beyond where I am currently educated will be me smiling and waving, which I am very good at, by the way. And sometimes, I've found, that's enough. Because, as my friend Tony wisely says, "Don't talk about it. Be about it."

Theory is just theory until you sow the seed, water and nourish it, harvest the fruit, and take a bite. The fruit from this Tree of Life is productive, delicious, and exciting, and generation-altering. I've taken these scientific assertions and mixed them with the truth of God's Word and applied them to daily living. They are working for me and my family in powerful and peaceful ways. That's fine by me. It's all by faith anyway. And faith moves mountains that science says are immovable. God is cool like that. That's the Good News of the Gospel!

"For we also have received the good news just as they did; but the message they heard did not benefit them, not being mixed with faith in those who heard it."
- Hebrews 4:2

With that said, let's entangle some science with faith, quantum-style.

Thank you for being here. This is so much fun to me. I hope you have fun, too!

The Lord made this for us.

Preface

Subatomic matter: the building blocks of all creation. Everything that was made is made from subatomic particles. In the beginning, God created the heavens and earth. The earth was without form, and the Spirit of God hovered over the surface of the waters: a vaporous cloud of subatomic matter.

The wind. The breath. The mind. The Spirit of Elohim.

Roo' Akh...

Roo' Akh...

Roooooooooooo' Aaaaaaaaaaakh...

The creative sound of the breath of God.

Rooooooooo' Aaaaaaaaaaaaaakhhhhhhhh...

Can you hear it?

The life-giving wind, blowing from the depths of the Creator...the Father... the Mother... the very Source of all that exists: Elohim.

God-breathed.

And the waters began to stir.

The dark, watery depths began to churn...

Can you feel the vibration?

Do you hear the brewing?

Can you see the sparks of light amidst the darkness from the friction?

This is how light was made:

The desire-filled energy of the Source of Power began to electrify atoms.

Electrons filled with excitement, spinning, faster and faster around the nuclei.

Protoplasm awakened, sensing commands, stood at attention, ready to receive information from the commander, awaiting final orders to BE.

And then, suddenly:

In a booming, explosive WORD, it happened:

"LIGHT: BE."

Electrons heard and felt it and LEAPT for joy, according to the command, jumping in and out of place, emitting bursts of electromagnetic energy:

LIGHT.

And it was so.

And Elohim looked upon it and spoke:

"It is Good."

And to this day, that WORD still travels beyond space and time, eventually collapsing upon itself, meeting its inevitable obsolescence:

His WORD will NOT return void; it will accomplish what He sent it forth to do.

There will be no need for light: For the Lord God will be your light.

"For I assure you: If you have faith the size of a mustard seed, you will tell this mountain, 'Move from here to there,' and it will move. Nothing will be impossible for you.
Matthew 17:20

Health. Relationships. Finances.

These are the three areas that any and every problem hits.

These are the three areas that we have great power to conform to the Will of God for our lives.

I know it doesn't seem that way; sometimes it feels like life has its way with us, to our despair.

But we know Jesus said that faith the size of a mustard seed could move mountains. He said that if we believe, nothing will be impossible for us. Because our faith speaks into the subatomic cloud of the womb of creation.

We believe; therefore, we speak. And then, we see.

He said He promised.

So, I believed Him.

And I put it to the test.

First, I tried commanding the mountains to move. And nothing happened.

Then, I tried speaking to dead trees to be raised back to life. No green in sight.

I tried manifesting luxury vehicles and fat bank accounts. I watched the test-driven Mercedes GLS drive back to the dealership, gone from my grasp. I was so close, but no. That bank account was still too skinny.

So, I thought, what if I tried speaking to something very small-something that wasn't impossible for humans to do, but I wanted to do it without "doing it." I had a spot on my forearm that appeared out of nowhere and looked suspicious. It absorbed all my attention for weeks as it continued to grow before my eyes. I decided to focus on commanding that to move- to be gone forever. I spoke to it daily for several months. As I did, I noticed it getting lighter, less raised. I kept at it, a little every day as I woke up in the morning. I would say, "Spot, be gone NOW, in Jesus' name, and never return." I also noticed the fear of what it "could be" was gone. It no longer terrorized me. I started to believe it was obeying me. Going, going, gone... it was almost gone.

One day, I was moving furniture. As I was squeezing a couch through my front door frame, a piece of flashing caught my arm and shaved a small, deep plug out of my arm, only and in the exact location as the spot.

And just like that, the remnant was totally gone, never to return. It was a clean cut, too- no scar. I can't even see now where it used to be.

I said, "God, that's cheating."

I mean, I could have gone to a doctor for that. I expected to see some huge, miraculous dissipation of genetic tissue scattering into thin air, and maybe the clouds would and a dove would fly down and land on me, with a voice from Heaven telling me how pleased God was with me and my faith.

Instead, He said, "No. I get my work done any way I like. That's how I did it that day."

I was just fine with that.

I can move that mountain by doctors in the first realm. I could move it by miracles from the second realm. Or I could just let God get it done however He chose to orchestrate it, from the third realm, from a position of rest. (You're gonna see what I'm talking about shortly. It's so fun!)

As the years passed, I continued to speak to things. Big things, little things, unimportant things, and urgent things. As I did, I often expected the huge fireworks show of miraculous display, but instead I'd just wake up one morning and realize the thing I was speaking to had been gone, sometimes for a while. I'd never even noticed- it was so gradual. I began to learn that once I commanded something to obey, it had to obey. And then, I could take my attention off it in full confidence and focus on more enjoyable things. Watching the desired outcome fall into place became like watching paint dry or a pot boil: the desired result was inevitable because God said so; watching it happen was a waste of time, and a threat to my faith. Because the watching caused the wavering: "did it work yet?", "Is it here yet?", "What's taking it so long?", "Will it even happen?", "Does this even work?" … My mom calls it, "giving it to God, and then taking it back again."

I'm thinking of the time Jesus commanded the fig tree to die. He cursed it, and walked on, not lingering to make sure it happened. Then, the next day, the disciples saw it shriveled up, and remembered what He said to it the day before. Jesus went on to tell them, if they had faith, they could speak to the mountain to be thrown into the sea, and it would obey. But He said they had to believe it would happen BEFORE it would happen. (Mark 11:22)

Finally, I realized: the big, miraculous display was never what God desired us to live on- miracles are for moments, like manna from heaven. They show us God's power and reveal His heart toward mankind. God is so kind and loving, like a good father, and meets us with His miracles exactly where we are in our weakest points. But we shouldn't need God to intercede for us in areas He told us to be the boss of. Jesus said, "an evil and adulterous generation demands a sign." (Matthew 16:4)

Instead, we are called to become mature believers who walk in faith and power, taking dominion of the earth as true sons of the living God. In that way, we become God's hands and feet, allowing His miraculous power to flow through us, for the good of all mankind. Jesus said so. The more we do it, the less it looks like a miracle. It makes the extraordinary become the ordinary day in the Kingdom: righteousness, peace, and joy on Earth as it already is in Heaven. As above, so below; no miracle needed because God's perfect will is always done.

A word of encouragement, however: even in our maturity, sometimes we get tired and lose focus. God is so good to meet us there with miracles, also. In our weakness, His power is shown. I'm seeing Elijah having just performed a mighty, miraculous act of God, receive a threat from Jezebel, and then collapse under a tree, begging God to kill him. God sends an angel to give him food that miraculously energizes him for forty more days. It reminds me of my early days with my skincare company, when I would crumble to the floor in emotional exhaustion at the slightest hint of failure, saying, "I quit. I'm done." My mom would look at me, roll her eyes, and tell me, "You can quit tomorrow. We have too much work to do today. Get up." And so I did…

Another interesting note about that moment with Elijah is that after the Lord miraculously strengthened him, it says Elijah kept going for forty days, and then ended up in a cave. Then the Lord came to Elijah and said, "What are you doing here?." What a great question we should ask ourselves when we are hiding, by the way. "What the heck am I doing here?!"

God told him to go outside. He needed to talk to Elijah- to open his eyes and ears and give him some fresh air. (That's also a great thing to do when we are hiding! Terror and fear cause us to lose our vision and our breath sometimes. Go outside. Get some fresh air and still those thoughts.)

Elijah obeyed, and he saw a strong wind tearing at the mountains. But God was not in the wind. Then an earthquake happened, and a fire, and the Lord wasn't in either of those. Finally, Elijah heard a small voice speaking, and he leaned in.

"What are you doing here?", God asked again, in a whisper. (I'm imagining this whole scene and I can see the Lord lean in really close, whispering that question gently, playfully, in a tone that exposes the obvious childishness of a mighty Man of God hiding in a cave.)

Of course, like I did every time I tried to justify wanting to quit my work, Elijah excused his behavior. I can also hear his tone in my mind, sounding like an oldest child who's been asked to gather his siblings and clean the house: "I did what you told me to do. Your kids are stupid and now they're trying to kill me. I'm staying away from them." (I paraphrased that response based on what I've heard a million times in my own house.)

Then God gave him instruction for his next steps. Just like that. No miracle, no mighty boom or display of power. Just a simple conversation: "Go. Now." (*I Kings 19*)

Sometimes that is a miracle in itself: that we can silence our fears, ego, and the enemy's noise enough to hear the Father, and then GET UP and do what we are instructed by God Himself to do.

They say, "you can't move a parked car." I say, "well, you can...you just have to lift it with a hoist and move it against its will." That's just annoying for everyone.

Every morning, Ponyo, my cat, sits on a dining chair in the kitchen, waiting for food. I make her food, show it to her, and take it to her eating spot. She remains on the chair, watching me move like I haven't fed her in days. So, I lift her up from the chair and carry her to the food. She gets annoyed at me every time and complains as I carry her. Then I put her down in front of her plate, and she walks to it as if it's the first she's heard about the food being there. I know she acts out the whole drama every day because she wants me to bring her food to her, in the exact spot she chose: the dining table for humans. I'm not doing it. She's a cat. She needs to go and do cat stuff, just as she was created to do. Not sit in a chair at our table, being lazy, getting her cat fur on all our food. She was made for more.

Don't be like Ponyo.

The "GO" is the whole point because the journey is what makes us become: Restored. Established. Strengthened. Supported.

And in the becoming, we are creating good fruit. Making more of the fruit. Filling the earth with our fruit. Subduing the ground we've been given.

In the doing, we are making Earth as it is in Heaven. Just as we were told to do: the will of The Father.

As I have continued to just "know" by faith, that God's promises will come to pass in my life as I continue to call them forth, the Lord continues to prove Himself over and over in every way. It allows me to take my eyes off the need and focus on the work I'm called to do on the planet. Because I know full well that whatever comes against His promises and the work He put in me to do, He will allow me to speak to it to force it to bow the knee to Him. Everything MUST obey the Lord. It can be no other way. And I know that I make it happen through my thoughts, emotions, words, and my actions.

Sometimes it happens immediately. And sometimes, it takes a while. But I am always sure: THAT mountain will be moved and scattered to dust.

A few years ago, my best friend, Amber, and I had gone to a cabin in the woods to pray for our families. We made a list of demands against mountains, so to speak, and began the process of causing the earth to submit to the will of God. On Earth, as it is in Heaven.

One of the commands was for any and every lie to be exposed and every lying spirit to leave our families. There were a couple of specific situations attached to that command, and we were focused on that being revealed and expelled. As soon as we started commanding, a very large snake slithered out from the fishing dock beneath us and swam as far away as it could. We were amazed at the symbolism of the snake exposing itself and exiting during that specific command but were even more thrilled to receive a phone call only moments later regarding that command. No one knew what we were praying about, but in an instant, as we were praying in a cabin two hours away, a lie was being exposed back at home, and the liar left suddenly on his own volition.

We rejoiced that day because we saw the instant manifestation of a mountain moved by our words. But we also know that sometimes, the mountains move inch by inch, indetectable at first, more noticeably altered next, and completely sunk in the end.

I've seen so much already:

- My own marriage rise from the ashes within a year.
- My children restored to the Light.
- Sicknesses and disorders in my body removed in a few months, weeks, days and hours of focused commands and praise.
- A knot on my son's head instantly gone the second my husband commanded it to go.
- Money manifested from the strangest places, in large sums, to cover future needs that we couldn't have covered on our own.
- Total hearing loss in one ear fully restored instantly.
- House sold in exactly the right time. Next house appeared the day we closed on our current house.
- Business sustained through every challenging time.
- Trips paid for supernaturally.
- Every financial need I've ever had: handled.
- Near-death Covid patient healed and back home in one week.
- Lifelong clinical depression healed instantly, for good.
- Tumors disappeared.
- Vehicles provided without cost.
- Disharmonious guests turning up their noses and walking away the instant we prayed for it to happen. (I've seen this several times.)
- Doors opened to heaven.
- Doors slammed shut to hell.

I've seen too much to doubt. I've seen so much: Healing and provision for relationships, health, and finances. All Covered. Sickness, poverty, brokenness: He's covered it all. It's part of the benefits of His insurance policy. (*Psalm 103*)

Covered. Covered. Covered. God had it all covered, exactly the way HE wanted it covered.

We know, no matter the how or how long, God's promises WILL come to pass: What we say, goes, when we say what HE says. It can be no other way. Jesus said so. I believe Him.

And because I believe Him, I see it constantly in my life: what I say according to the will of God, goes. Many people say they never see it, or it doesn't work that way. They don't see it because they don't believe it. Or when it does happen, they chalk it up to coincidence or inevitability. Or they don't recognize it because it came wrapped in a different package. (I know- I've done that myself.) EVERY good gift comes from above. EVERY GOOD GIFT. We praise Him for it all. And they also don't practice it. Again and again, practice. Diligently practice faith. Like doctors practice medicine and athletes practice their sport and see greater results as they continuously put their hands to the work, so we practice faith in Jesus and power in that name, in any area of our lives and see better results as we continuously put our hearts and minds and words and deeds to work.

I like how my sister, Tracy describes it: Grit.

Sometimes, it takes grit to stay the course and believe what you cannot yet see. Grit those eyes. Grit those teeth. Grit those fists. Grit your feet with spikes into the ground. Get tough. Do. Not. Move.

I often take a "Superwoman" position when I feel the thoughts of failure and fear come upon me. I put my hands on my hips, standing with feet firmly planted, and I say to the thought, sometimes in a VERY loud voice, mostly so my ego hears it, "You WILL obey me." And then, I force it to obey.

"Now without faith it is impossible to please God, for the one who draws near to Him must believe that He exists and rewards those who seek Him."
Hebrews 11:6

Practice makes the perfect come. It flows from the subatomic realm into the visible realm.

I heard Ed Mylett speak about an earthly law he calls "The Law of Compound Pounding": Consistent hitting of the thing weakens the thing until it eventually must yield to you. Hit it again. Hit it again. Hit it again. Hit it again. Hit it again. Hit it again. Hit it again. Hit it again. Hit it till you get it.

The time it takes matters not. There is a season for it all. And like a good farmer, I dream it up. I till the soil. I sow it into the ground. I water it and nourish it to life. I collect the harvest. And then, I rest. All the while, the Lord God breathes into the soil, into the seed, into the ether, into the matter, into the souls, into every quantum particle to cause it all to come to life. We co-create together through Subatomic Faith.

First, we see it in the mind. Then, we feel it in the heart. Next, we speak it through the vibrations of light and sound. And finally, we hold it in our hands: waves collapsed into matter.

We see it, and say, "It is good."

On Earth as it is in Heaven.

To the glory of God and to the expansion of His Kingdom.

So be it.

Acknowledgement

In the words of Matthew McConaughey, "Gratitude Reciprocates."

Thanks and acknowledgment to the following people for helping this book come to life:

Of course, my husband, Aaron Lehmann. You are my muse, protector, my very own in-house Rock Star. That guitar in your hands will get you out of any trouble with me. I'm your biggest fan. I love you. Thank you for believing the weird stuff and living it out. This is so much fun.

My sweet tiny baby children: I know you didn't ask to be born, but here we are. 😊 You nuggets are troopers- those summer days on the ladders with paintbrushes are paying off. With great attitudes, you lived through the push, and now, we get to REALLY enjoy ourselves together. To the victors go the spoils.

My parents: You two are the whole image of the masculine and feminine aspects of God; you both make it easy to trust HIM because of it. Thank you for loving me the way you do, and for supporting my family as we took this path.

Tom and Sue Lehmann: The Pioneers. You carved a different path for your family, disregarding what others thought. Grace, freedom, and truth are your legacy to us.

Andrea Calvery: the art that flows through you now flows through me. Thank you for your expansive generosity and your love for God's people. You are a Ruler.

Krista Dunk @ 100X Publishing: Always helpful, extremely knowledgeable: thank you for all the advice and help with this work. You rescued me for sure.

Introduction: God Said Write. NOW.

In the fall of 2019, I had a bizarre dream about a mother and her children that left me interested in its interpretation. I wrote down the details as soon as I woke up and pondered them for a few days after. By the third day, the Lord showed me clearly what it meant. I digested it all, took it to a livestream teaching on social media, and enjoyed sharing how cool God was (is) to give us plenty of tools to live the abundant life we are called to live in THIS time on Earth. We won't need them later, in the Restoration of All Things. But for now- we need all the help we can get.

At the time, I was focused on the warfare aspect of it all: I felt like the dream gave me a blueprint of how to cast off those demons of thought that plague our minds and wreak havoc on our bodies through depression, addiction, sickness, self-sabotage, abuse, broken relationships, poverty, and overall unwellness. That's where my focus was at that time: casting off what doesn't belong to or on me and my loved ones.

But today, as I was meditating in the secret place with the Lord, He reminded me of the dream, telling me to write it as a guide RIGHT NOW, and He would show me what to do with it after I finished. As I rewatched the video just now, I can see that my earlier focus was myopic. Warfare wasn't the big picture of the dream. The MOTHER was. The mother and her ability to birth life and freedom into the earth- that was the message of the dream.

So here I am, laying aside plans for the moment, in full confidence that He is going to collapse time and space for me to start and finish quickly. We'll see what we do with it after it's written. I already know it will be exceedingly, abundantly beyond all I was thinking of, or could even know to ask.

He is a Good Father.

I have a feeling He's about to show us how to be a good mother (you guys, too!)- how to birth HIS plans, dreams, and FUN STUFF into the world, bypassing the residual waste that comes with having to "take the good with the bad" during manifesting. He's about to show us how to manifest Jesus-style.

As I use terms like "woman" and "mother", understand that in this case, I am using them as metaphors for the feminine energy of every person, male and female, that the Lord uses to conceive, protect, birth and nurture life inside us all. And know that when God told Adam and Eve from the beginning: be fruitful, multiply, fill the earth and take dominion over it, He didn't just mean to make a bunch of babies. He was speaking to ALL fruit- every good thing that flows from our flesh. The life and blessings that flow from us all: to the Glory of God.

Also note that throughout the book, I will quote scriptures from the Bible. Sometimes I will give the exact location. Other times, I'll cite the entire chapter. This is so that you can see the full context of the idea and take a journey into the mind and heart of God and His creation. His character is found in the stories- you'll get to know His ways more intimately.

Let's do it.

1

The Dream

"The Grand Illusion"

Masked as beauty, humor and mystique, the mime presents the lustre.
Smoke and mirrors. Dust and glitter. A cloud of heaviness for clout.
But we fear not, nor are we amused, its illusion does not pass the muster.
We see through its lies, its attempt to decieve; with a finger, we cast it out.

The dream began on my childhood street, in front of my house. Standing behind me were people I consider my prayer partners- my daughter, sister, several of my friends, my mom-in-law- and my husband. My mom approached me, looking bewildered, and she said, "I have a child being born in there (pointing to our house) that I didn't even know about." She was shocked about it, wondering how she could birth a child she didn't know of. As I looked at her, obviously not pregnant and not in labor in that house, since she was standing in front of me, I said, "No." She was puzzled, unconvinced. I repeated it: "No. Nah. You're not." Then I turned to my crew and motioned them to follow me. They formed a "V" behind me, and we all went into the house to check it out.

Upon entering the front room, on the left side against the wall was a bassinet with a baby in it. I approached the baby to inspect and saw it: it was short in length like a newborn, yet had an overgrown, bald head of an old man, a shriveled face, evil eyes, and the rolls of a small, morbidly obese baby. It was not human, not a true newborn, and was being completely neglected in the corner of the room.

I looked at it, rolled my eyes, and said, "NO."

Then I turned and walked to the mother.

On the far right side of the room was the "mother": lying on a gurney, pretending to writhe in pain (I could tell it was faking because in between moans, it would look at me to make sure I was noticing its performance). It was also not a true mother: it was male, short like a gnome, but had facial features that were animalistic. As it moaned and gazed over to me, I at once said to it, "NO."

It stopped moaning and said, "Is she allowed to be in here?" while looking over its shoulder. I noticed a hazy figure to my right, at the head of the "mother". She was its nurse, and she was checking stats and vitals on a machine and trying to speak to me. I could barely see or hear her, but she was timid and very much getting on my nerves.

I focused sharply on the "mother" again. When I did, I realized it was staring at my daughter, who was standing on my left side, and she was becoming drowsy. I immediately covered her eyes, gave it a look of warning, and then said, "Do you know Jesus?"

The "mother" looking victimized at the nurse again, said, "Is she allowed to say these things to me?"

The nurse tried to speak again while fiddling with the equipment, and mumbling in agreement with the mother. I was done with her.

I looked in her direction and said, "You don't even matter. Shut up." With one hand, I swatted her away and she was gone.

The "mother" then sat up and fixed on my daughter again. It jumped up on the bed, now eye-level with us, and blew a dusty, dirty golden glitter at her face, in an attempt to enchant her with its beauty.

Extremely irritated with these tactics, I put my left arm around my daughter's shoulder, drew her closer to me, and covered her eyes again with my left hand. With my right hand, I easily swatted the dusty glitter away and decided I'd had enough.

On my right side were all my prayer partners. I quickly lined them up and said, "Worship the Lord NOW!" They all began shouting, stomping, praising and clapping, and laughing in joy. The floor began vibrating: the sounds of a mighty army marching toward the battle line- the room was filled with the sounds of victory. The "mother" started jumping up and down, screaming like a monkey.

I looked at it and began the indictment:

You have tormented my family for too long.
You have killed billions with your lies and manipulations.
You have stolen identities and replaced them with counterfeits.
You have robbed and destroyed what is rightfully ours and NOT yours.
You have influenced and enchanted the innocent and caused their demise.
You are GUILTY of crimes against humanity.
I convict you and send you out NOW.
Go to hell and never return. And take that baby with you.
NOW! In Jesus' name!

4

And with that, it was gone.
  And then I woke up.

2

Historical Set-Up

"Dwelling Place"

Where could I go from your presence, Lord.
Where could I flee from your Spirit.
No matter where I hide, you are there.
You are knitting me together in the womb of
creation;
You never stop molding me, expanding me, loving
me, making me:
I dwell with you.

In order to reveal the interpretation, I must make sure you know the story of Abraham, Sarah, and their sons.

Follow me as I lay down the path.

Abraham and Sarah are historical figures in the Old Testament, appearing first in Genesis 12, and then flooding the entire Old and New Testament, along with the Quran, with children...heirs.

The couple were pagans who worshiped many gods until the Lord Jehovah called them out of their land, and into a journey of faith with Him.

He promised to bless them with a multitude of children (including the Messiah) and property, yet several years into the promise, they had not yet conceived a child. So, Sarah decided to take matters into her own hands and get the job done her way. She directs Abraham to take her servant, Hagar, and make a baby with her. He agrees, it is done, and Ishmael is conceived. Once pregnant, Hagar begins to disrespect Sarah and treat her with malice, and Sarah becomes bitter against Abraham for it (?!?!) Abraham tells Sarah to do whatever she wants to Hagar (?!?!!!), so Sarah makes life unbearable for Hagar. Hagar runs away, then comes back. Finally, the child God had planned for Sarah is born through Sarah's once barren womb: Isaac. Ishmael spends many years harassing baby brother Isaac, and Sarah has had enough. She wants them to GO. The Lord tells Abraham to listen to his wife and send Hagar and Ishmael on their way- He promises to care for them and bless them, too, and does. And so it goes.

There is much more to this story, and it can be found in Genesis 16, but it's all we need to know for the dream set-up.

3

The Interpretation

"Daughter"

I am the fruit of Truth; I bear the fruit of Life;
I multiply the fruit of Freedom
to the ends of the earth.

A s I pondered the meaning behind the dream, I kept thinking about my mom, that distorted child next to my child, and the harassing "mother." The two moms and the thought, "harassing" caught my attention. There, the Lord reminded me of a scripture in Galatians 4:

For it is written that Abraham had two sons, one by a slave and the other by a free woman. But the one by the slave was born according to the impulse of the flesh, while the one by the free woman was born as the result of a promise.

These things are illustrations, for the women represent the two covenants.

One is from Mount Sinai and bears children into slavery—this is Hagar.

Now Hagar is Mount Sinai in Arabia and corresponds to the present Jerusalem,

for she is in slavery with her children. But the Jerusalem above is free, and she is our mother. For it is written:

Rejoice, childless woman,

who does not give birth.

Burst into song and shout,

you who are not in labor,

for the children of the desolate are many,

more numerous than those

of the woman who has a husband.

Now you, brothers, like Isaac, are children of promise. But just as then the child born according to the flesh persecuted the one born according to the Spirit, so also now.

But what does the Scripture say?

Drive out the slave and her son, for the son of the slave will never be a coheir with the son of the free woman.

Therefore, brothers, we are not children of the slave but of the free woman.

As we look back at the characters of the dream, we note the following players:

- My mom.
- Me.
- My daughter.
- My mother's alleged newborn child of another mother.
- A false mother.
- A nurse.
- My prayer partners.

Much like the story of Abraham, Sarah and the two sons, the dream is an allegory of manifesting desires according to the will of God versus the will of man.

My mother represented Sarah, the free woman who is called to birth children (life, dreams, ideas, promises, seed, actual children) into freedom. She was confused that she could have born a child and not know it. I was her child, and she knew me. That child did not come through her.

I represented the "child of the promise," the free child- Isaac. I understood who I was, who my mother was, who the fake "mother" and nurse were, and who the newborn child was NOT. To every lie, I said, "No." I didn't even entertain it. I knew the truth, even as the lies tried to persuade me otherwise.

My daughter represented every generational heir of the promise of God- Abraham's true children: Protected, covered, kept safe and hidden from attacks. Free to Become. Free to birth life into freedom: dreams, ideas, actual children, entire life destinies.

The newborn "child" represented the "child of the flesh"- like the Ishmael allegory, it was a manifested creation conceived of fleshly desires, born outside of the promise of God, and driven by a person's own will to manifest, no matter who or what has to participate to make it happen. It is born into slavery to the will of its creator and always looks like a distortion of what was meant to be, a slave to the unjust laws of man, whose fruit leads to death. It is unloved and neglected of light and life and love and freedom to prosper. We'll talk more about this child in a moment.

The false "mother," the slave woman, was easy to recognize: It was our evil desires. We could also call it the devil, or demons that attempt to plague our minds. It was a counterfeit "mother" attempting to birth life where only death can result. It was false in every way: not a woman, not actually in pain, acting like a victim but was the source of the trouble, trying to seduce the innocent ones with dirty, dusty magic, jumping around, screaming as if it had any true power, easy to expel when exposed.

The nurse: when God showed me who she represented, it really took me by surprise.

Watch how this one unfolded; God is so cool.

> *No one undergoing a trial should say, "I am being tempted by God." For God is not tempted by evil, and He Himself doesn't tempt anyone. But each person is tempted when he is drawn away and enticed by his own evil desires. Then after desire has conceived, it gives birth to sin, and when sin is fully grown, it gives birth to death.*
>
> *Don't be deceived, my dearly loved brothers. Every generous act and every perfect gift is from above, coming down from the Father of lights; with Him there is no variation or shadow cast by turning.*
>
> *James 1:13-17*

The nurse was our own flesh that coddles our evil/ selfish desires. The nurse is that part of us that tries to justify, convince, and protect our self-will, when we know deep within that what we want is spiritually, ethically, physically, or morally destructive. The nurse caves to temptation. She is only as strong as her host allows her to be, and without her, the fake "mother" cannot even stay. The nurse is our own EGO. A powerful point: the nurse nurtures the desire, not the produce of it. Notice in my dream, no one was taking care of the "child"- it was left to die. The nurse focused on the feigned needs of the "mother", who, in reality, had no needs at all, and needed to be cast out. Simultaneously, the "mother" wanted the nurse to protect it, nurse it, and give it validation. Remember how it kept looking at the nurse, asking if I had the right to be there and speak?

And remember how easy it was for me to dismiss the nurse? When she was shut down, IT was shut down. For good.

The nurse is the first person to look at when there's a problem in your life.

Shut her DOWN.

The Lord revealed much through the nurse, I believe to show us how much control over our own lives we truly have. We often blame Satan or others or "bad luck/ fate" for the trouble in the world and surrender to fear, abuse, and temptation because of it. But the reality is: evil and his cohort are OUR prisoners, we are NOT their prisoners. We have been given power and authority to overrule evil. The nurse within us needs to be fired- she's the one unlocking evil's chains. *(Colossians 2:15)* This includes our flesh. We are the bosses of our own desires.

Here is what the nurse helps deliver into your world, through the slave woman's body:

Now the works (*birth) of the flesh are obvious: sexual immorality, moral impurity, promiscuity, idolatry, sorcery, hatreds, strife, jealousy, outbursts of anger, selfish ambitions, dissensions, factions, envy, drunkenness, carousing, and anything similar. I tell you about these things in advance—as I told you before—that those who practice such things will not inherit the Kingdom of God.
Galatians 5:16-21
(*I added "birth" for parallel)

We'll look at what it means to miss the inheritance of the Kingdom of God in a bit. But let's draw a clearer picture of what the nurse, the slave woman, and the slave child produce together.

In a flow chart, it looks like this:

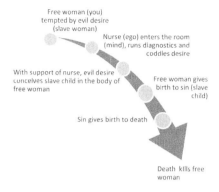

The "slave woman" (evil desires/ temptation to do evil) enters in either by invitation of the "free woman" (true children of God) or through self-insertion, without permission. She tempts the free woman with an evil desire. The free woman calls for the nurse, who immediately hooks her body up to machines to run diagnostics, revealing she did need that (fill-in-the-blank) temptation after all, because she was the victim- someone hurt her or left her out or stole from her or ignored her or abandoned her. The free woman may rationalize that she always gets the short end of the stick, everything bad always happens to her, she never wins, she deserves it, has waited long enough, etc... So, she decides with the nurse's hearty approval, to be drawn away with the temptation. She conceives desire in that moment. As the desire grows in the womb, the nurse is there, coddling the decision and her actions, until sin is born into the world. When sin grows up, it always produces the fruit of death.

What does a fully grown evil desire (the baby of the slave woman) look like?

The fruit of evil: broken relationships, destroyed families, murder, rape, sexual immorality, human trafficking, disease, addiction, poverty, homelessness, incarceration, abuse, mental illness, racism, sexism, classism, injustice of all sorts, genocide, oppression, death of all sorts.

Instead, as the nurse is cast out, and the Spirit of God is allowed to nurture the flesh, the fruit of the Spirit is born:

But the fruit of the Spirit is love, joy, peace, patience, kindness, goodness, faithfulness, gentleness, self-control. Against such things there is no law.
(Galatians 5:22-23)

What does the Fruit of the Spirit, fully grown, look like?

Healed relationships, strong families, full of life, sexual wholeness, value for human life, healthy bodies, moderation, wealthy, housed and fed, free to be, confident, competent, respectful of self and others, just, merciful, generous, life-giving in every way.

Notice again that scripture in James about the cycle of evil desires:

Don't be deceived, my dearly loved brothers. Every generous act and every perfect gift is from above, coming down from the Father of lights; with Him there is no variation or shadow cast by turning.
James 1:13-17

I find it extremely interesting that it begins with: "Don't be deceived, dearly loved brothers."

He says that every GOOD gift comes from above, coming down from the Father of Lights. The TRUE gifts and blessings that come from God don't come with shifting or shadows.

Remember in the Garden of Eden, there were two trees: the Tree of the Knowledge of Good and Evil, and the Tree of Life.

They were instructed to take only from the Tree of Life: it yielded ONLY LIFE. That means wins for all who partook.

Eating the fruit from the Tree of the Knowledge of Good and Evil was forbidden because it allowed humankind to be exposed to both good and evil. It allowed ulterior intentions to enter their lives. As I write this, I'm thinking of how a parent forbids certain types of content for their young children: it opens their eyes to things they should never have to see because it impacts the soul.

> " *The blessings of the Lord it, maketh rich, and He addeth no sorrow with it."*
> *Proverbs 10:22 (KJV)*

The fruit of that tree offers a scale: in the short term, someone wins, and someone loses as they weigh the good versus the bad- the blessings and curses. But in the end, everyone who takes from this tree loses. It produces the fruit of death every time. There is an expression that says, "You can pay on the front end, or you can pay on the back end. Either way, you're going to pay."

When dealing with the Tree of the Knowledge of Good and Evil, you will always pay. It's just a matter of when and how much. And the "how much" is almost always disproportionately higher than the fruit consumed. All creation groans with labor pains, waiting to be set free from these laws.

When we take from the Tree of Life, there is no payment due. The bill has already been paid in full. Everyone who takes from it lives abundantly and has access to every good gift in abundance. If the gift/ prayer/ desire you give or receive has shadows or shifting, it's not from above- it's from flesh and it brings death. It's not worth it. Cast it away.

Start with the nurse. She's a "NO." She doesn't even matter. *Don't let her affect your matter.*

Once we send her away, getting rid of the slave woman is easy- She can't stay where she is not nourished. Look to the prayer partners, and then take your position.

And finally, the prayer partners in the dream represent those you are in agreement with, who love the Lord and are called to His purposes, not their own fears and biases. They pray the will of God to come to pass, "On Earth as it is in Heaven". Notice the approach they took in the dream: as we entered the house, they automatically formed a "V" behind me. Metaphorically, it suggests that together, we will expend less energy on the job we were about to perform, making the task easy, and be able to ascend higher, faster. Also, note in the dream: no one was scared or worried or tried to talk me out of anything- no one doubted that victory was mine. No one warned me that they'd seen this thing before, and it was hard to beat. No one told me to pray for the best but expect the worst. No one suggested that perhaps it was God's will for the slave woman to have her way with my daughter. No one suggested that we should take the matter to a priest or pastor or doctor or counselor or someone higher.

Instead, like when the courageous Israelite army took Jericho, they praised and rejoiced and celebrated BEFORE the false mother was expelled. They were confident in God's competence to perform what He said He could do through us. And He did, easily. Make sure that your militia is courageous and filled with faith; A doubtful prayer partner can become "friendly fire" in your troop- not everyone knows how to pray for you or with you according to the will and Word of God, and words create worlds. Jesus put doubtful people out of the room as He was getting ready to raise a girl from the dead. (Of course, He could get the job done regardless, but I'm guessing they were getting on His nerves.)

Journal Entry

The world lets demons have too much freedom on this planet.
Many aren't even aware of the spiritual war that goes on in the second
realm, and even those who profess to follow Jesus dismiss their existence,
ignoring the fact that a huge part of His work on Earth dealt with
setting people free from demonic influence. His last words to the
disciples before He went back to the throne were to cast out demons in
His name- He said that ability was a sign that followed the ones who

believed Him (Mark 16:17). That means, if we aren't able to get demons off people, we don't believe Him. It also means demons are real. I'm not sure how or why this fact was lost on Christians around the world, especially in America and Europe. Head to Africa or South America, and I promise you, you will find a substantial number of people who know how real demons are, and how destructive they can be if allowed to run amuck by humans. My friend, Kathryn Shindoll was a missionary in Zambia for a decade, and she worked with orphans daily. She said that demonic influence over the kids was so common that they performed demonic deliverances regularly. In fact, many of the orphans were spiritually, physically, sexually, and mentally abused by witch doctors; They were used for trafficking and satanic rituals. Demonic oppression was common knowledge in the land. Her staff just cast the demons out as the children came into the school where she served. We should do the same.

A great tip and teaching that I have heard from one of my favorite teachers on the subject, and my missionary friend agreed, is to not allow demons to throw a fit or take up attention. Just as Jesus did during His ministry, we are shown to command the demons to be silent and come out. To let them writhe and dramatize and throw fits and such is to give them illegitimate power over the situation, to cause fear and awe at the demon's power among the audience, and to prolong the torment of the poor soul being used as a host. Set the souls free NOW. Anything less is pride and cruelty.

4

The TRUE Mother Births Life into Freedom

"MOTHER"

Veins like rivers...
Sending and receiving.
Downloading...Uploading.
Jumping off...Jumping in.
Diving, swimming, floating...
Center, outlander.
Lover, fighter, winner, ruler.

My true mother had a hard childhood- she grew up in a mentally, sexually, and physically abusive home. I grew up hearing the stories. She told them not from a position of victimization, but from a perspective of love: she always spoke highly of her parents, despite their abuse toward the children. But my siblings and I were never subject to them as children- she and my dad kept us safe from potential harm they could cause us. During her stories, she always said that God had protected her from ever knowing hatred in her heart. She said she only felt sad for them that they hadn't experienced the true love that God gives.

She told me the stories to show me the choices we had the power to make within our own lives, and that we could be victims, or we could be conquerors. She chose to conquer. She has never been a victim.

And as a result, my siblings and I were born into freedom. We've never known abuse, addiction, murder, rape, abandonment, trafficking, or hatred in our hearts...nothing of the sort. We were free to be children, playing safely, full of imagination, full of creativity, full of possibilities. It's no coincidence that all three of us are entrepreneurs- we've always been drawn to freedom.

Christmas morning was always exciting in our home. We were not financially wealthy by any means, but mom made every small gift seem like a treasure, carefully wrapped, and piled under the tree. Even things like crayons and paper were individually wrapped! My siblings and I would wake up at 5 am, and sit at the door of our rooms, literally shaking, and our teeth chattering from excitement, waiting for our parents to escort us to the tree!

When I was about 11 years old, as we were all unwrapping our gifts, I was overcome with love for my mom and her love for us. It struck me suddenly that she had never experienced anything like that with her own mother, and it filled me with sadness for her. I asked her, "Mom, do you wish you had a mom who did all this for you when you were a child?"

Her response: "I became the mom I always wanted. My heart is full."

She continued to say, repeatedly my entire life, "You aren't responsible for the things people do to you. You are only responsible for how you respond to them, and to yourself. And to God"

And as I write this, I am hearing this truth:

To react is to give away your power. To respond is to wield your
power.

My mother let go of the past and moved forward with God. Many things were thrown at her as we grew up, but she always responded in truth, disregarding the nurse and the false mother- a slave child was never born through her. We are a whole family to this day because of it. And we will continue to be whole if we follow her lead.

The free woman responds with power to bring forth life. The enslaved woman relinquishes power through her flesh and brings forth death.

So, the question is: what is the purpose of a mother?

A mother conceives a new life apart from her own. She protects life in her womb. She builds it a home. At the appointed time, she births life out of darkness, then she brings it into the light.

**She lets the past pass. She creates in the present. She establishes
the future.**

Like wisdom, she is the architect of the world she wants to live in. *(Proverbs 8:22-31)*

She co-creates with the builder, Elohim. On Earth, as it is in Heaven.

As above, so below.

Look at how the Lord birthed creation into existence in the beginning:

*In the beginning God created the heavens and the earth. Now the earth
was formless and empty, darkness covered the surface of the watery
depths, and the Spirit of God was hovering over the surface of the*

waters. Then God said, "Let there be light," and there was light. God saw that the light was good, and God separated the light from the darkness. God called the light "day," and He called the darkness "night." Evening came and then morning: the first day.

Genesis 1

Here we see Elohim God (the Trinity) hovering, like a mother giving birth, over the surface of the watery darkness. He spoke into the darkness, and light became. He named it: first evening came (dark), and then morning (light).

We birth into darkness and bring the fruit into the light. First dark, then light.

Our natural children are birthed in the watery darkness of the womb and brought into the light of the natural world.

Our dreams, ideas, hopes, and plans are born in the watery depths of the mind and brought into the light of the manifested realm.

We think about a thing. We labor in the darkness. Then we hold it in our hands, lifting our child into the light of life.

We conceive new life apart from our own. We protect life in our wombs. We build it a home.

At the appointed time, we birth life out of darkness, then we bring it into the light.

We let the past pass. We create in the present. We establish the future.

We are the architects of the world we want to live in.

We birth children into freedom.

According to the natural and spiritual laws that established Heaven and Earth, ***truth is the governor of freedom****. (John 8:32)*

As we walk in truth, we stay free, and we birth children into freedom.

5

The Slave Woman Births Life into Slavery

"Rise"

Your time of strife must end;
You have ended.
Now, flow; Let us carry you above.
Come where we are.
Your time of love must begin;
You have begun.
Just come.

Together, we create anew.

M any are familiar with Sarah's story, and how Ishmael and the troubles surrounding his birth came to be. But the story is common, where we humans are continuously offered freedom to grow and thrive but habitually enslave ourselves.

If we survey our memories, we'll recall areas where perhaps we felt victimized or left out. We blame others or God and stew on what we perceive as attacks that hold us back. But as we do, we become captive to our own imaginary limitations and envy. We struggle to succeed. We become a slave woman, birthing "children" into slavery.

But what is the cause of any of our enslavement?

This is what I hear, loud and clearly:

> *What is the source of wars and fights among you? Don't they come from*
> *the cravings that are at war within you? You desire and do not have.*
> *You murder and covet and cannot obtain. You fight and war. You do*
> *not have because you do not ask. You ask and don't receive because you*
> *ask with wrong motives, so that you may spend it on your evil desires.*
> *James 4:1-3*

We desperately want the things we do not have. We set our hearts on obtaining at any cost. We don't ask, and then are upset when we don't receive. But when we do ask, we ask with the wrong motives- to feed our evil desires.

I'm thinking about a woman I knew once who had knowingly started an affair with a married man. The feelings she felt were powerful, and the story he was telling her made her feel alive and seen, perhaps for the first time ever. As she was describing the story, she said that she knew that the Lord had sent him because of the intense "love" (passion) they felt for each other. She said she had prayed for him to come- they were even secretly going to church together and getting counseling from the pastor, who didn't know he was married. She completely disregarded the fact that he had a wife who was blindsided and devastated by the news, and their marriage was destroyed. The adulterous couple, of course, didn't make it much further after his divorce. Death was imminent. She claimed he was a gift from God, but she was deceived: that gift had shadows all around it. He was not her gift from above. He was a manifested desire born from their flesh into bondage. That relationship had death all over it.

That is what the scriptures mean by "every good gift comes from above, with no shadows or shiftiness." The caution says, "Do not be deceived." Apparently, we needed that caution to be able to spot a good gift from God versus a gift manifested from our own evil desires.

So, how do we avoid these cravings that are at war within us?

The scripture above follows:

God resists the proud but gives grace to the humble. Submit to God.
Resist the Devil, and he will flee from you. Draw near to God, and He
will draw near to you.
James 4:6

Remember the fake mother from my dream? Cast her out. Tell her to go, and take her nasty, shriveled death-child with her. She will go, I promise. She must.

Remember the nurse who coddles desires and offenses, and doesn't give a flip about the life she is bringing into the world? Remember that death-baby in the corner of the room that was being neglected and unloved? The nurse doesn't care about that. The nurse always only cares about the slave woman and its cravings. The girl and guy in the affair didn't care about the "life" they were trying to produce any more than they cared about the life they destroyed. When we rage and destroy, we rarely look back at the destruction we've caused- the nurse within us coddles our actions and feelings, justifying it all. The nurse is NOTHING but our own ego and pride. God resists her. So should we. "Make no provisions for the flesh, to satisfy its desires." (*Romans 13:14*)

When we do, grace flows, and we are free in our own hearts to draw near to God, to care about what God cares about, and to bring to life the things

God wants to birth into this Earth realm through us.

This is how we avoid enslaving ourselves, and this is how we birth true children into the freedom of Heaven on Earth: as above, so below.

This is what God meant for us to do from the very beginning of mankind:

Be fruitful. Multiply your fruit. Fill the earth with fruit. Take dominion over your territory.

We are free to be free.

We choose it.

6

The Three Realms

"Ray of Hope"

The light shines in the darkness, and the darkness
cannot overcome it.
I absorb the light and let it change me.
Forever illuminated by Hope.
Forever radiating His Power.

I'd like to take a closer look at those two trees in the garden again. As described earlier, we know that one tree produced fruit that gave life, and another tree produced fruit that yielded good AND evil.

We were advised to take from one and leave the other alone. But we ask ourselves, "what harm could there be in having knowledge, weighing 'good versus bad', pros and cons, and selecting accordingly?

After all, doesn't it say somewhere, "My people perish for lack of knowledge?"

It would seem that way. But context is everything.

May I show you another angle?

*A house is **built** by **wisdom**,*
*and it is **established** by **understanding**;*
*by **knowledge** the **rooms are filled***
*with **every precious and beautiful treasure**.*
Proverbs 24:3-4

Imagine with me three circles:

The first circle is "Earth"- the created, visible realm where we exist. This is the realm where we live in the flesh, and everything that we have created comes to life, manifested for good or evil. It is founded by wisdom (or lack thereof, according to each inhabitant) and is extremely pliable. It exists according to the thoughts and will of the observer, is experienced differently for each person, and can change in a moment.

In this realm, Earth, facts rule. Founded by **wisdom**, or lack thereof.

The second circle is "the heavens"- the created, invisible realm where demons and angels operate, where powers and principalities oversee and spiritual battles are fought (*Ephesians 6:12, Revelations 12*), and where all quantum matter exists. Genesis 1 says in the beginning, the Spirit of God was hovering over the surface of this realm- the waters; This is the spiritual realm where everything is created- the "womb" of manifestation. Our souls create here: mind, will and emotions. This realm is established by understanding according to each creator.

In this realm, possibilities rule. Established by **understanding**, or lack thereof.

The third circle is "the Kingdom of God"- the eternal realm that we were created to live in as co-creators and rulers with Elohim God. This is the realm where God dwells and where His will is known, performed, and fixed forever. This is the place that Jesus spoke about, "On Earth as it is in Heaven"- it is the permanent abode of God and man, and God's perfect will for each person has already been lived out here. Our spirit lives here when we are in Christ. By knowledge, everything a person needs and desires flows out from this realm: it gushes forth in abundance, bringing about the Perfect Will of God for mankind: "On Earth as it is in Heaven." It is also the place Jesus spoke about when He said, "seek first the Kingdom of God and its righteousness, and then everything will be added to you." *(Matthew 6:33)*

In this realm, truth rules. Filled with rich and precious treasures, accessible to all by knowledge.

Now, let's imagine each of the circles as a flat sphere, with the first circle, "Earth" on the bottom, the second circle, "Heaven" in the middle, and the third circle, "the Kingdom of God" on top.

We saw that wisdom founds the earth, understanding establishes the heavens, and knowledge of the Kingdom gives people everything they need and desire to do the work they are called to do on this earth.

We know that the book of Genesis says in the beginning, the earth (first realm) was formless and void. The Spirit of God (third realm) was hovering over the surface of the waters (second realm).

Then God, from the third realm SPOKE into the second realm, where all subatomic matter exists, and said, "Let there be light".

And it was so: Light became and pushed through the fabric of the second realm into the first realm, and it was seen. And it was good.

With wisdom, understanding, and knowledge, the world and all it contains was built, established, and filled to overflowing.

It was first desired in the third realm by the knowledge of God. Next, it was conceived and spoken into existence into the second realm by understanding. Finally, it was held in the hands, clearly seen and existing in the first realm by wisdom.

> *The Lord **founded** the earth by **wisdom***
> *and **established** the heavens by **understanding**.*
> *By His **knowledge** the **watery depths broke open**,*
> *and the **clouds dripped with dew**.*
> *Proverbs 3:19, 20*

Every good and perfect gift flows down from above. Everything is created in the spirit before it exists in the flesh.

We are called to create in the same manner:

Just as carnal knowledge is the desire that initiates conception in a womb, resulting in the manifested reality of that desire, so spiritual knowledge is the desire that initiates conception in the womb of creation, resulting in the manifested reality of that desire.

> *To say it most bluntly: sexual desire makes babies. Spiritual desire*
> *makes babies, too.*

We conceive in the third realm by the knowledge of God. We speak it into existence by understanding in the second realm. We hold it in our hands by wisdom in the first realm.

There is a way to create from the first realm (earth) only, by ignoring the second realm (the heavens) and the third realm (Kingdom of God).

There is also a way to create from the first realm (earth) into the second (the heavens), bypassing the third realm (the Kingdom of God.)

These two ways are how most humans (roughly 98%) create.

We were never meant to create without the third realm because the third realm is where the PERFECT gifts from God exist: the good, pleasing, and perfect will of God for us.

Just for example, here's what each scenario could look like, in general:

Let's say we have the desire to repair a relationship. We decide to take action.

Creating from Earth only (the first realm):

You are on the earth and have an offense against someone. You think, "If I can communicate how they made me feel and the wrong they caused, perhaps they will be moved with compassion or guilt and apologize to me. Then, I will feel better, and we can move forward.

You collect yourself, connect with the person, explaining your position in hopes that they will see things your way, and all will be restored.

They look at you like you grew a second head, wondering how the heck you totally dismissed your role in the relational demise, and walk away, assuming you are delusional, narcissistic, or just plain dumb.

OR- they go passive, let you pass the blame wholly onto them, and apologize just to make peace, knowing they can't fully trust you or have a truly unconditional relationship with you. They know you will never allow them to express themselves openly.

In this scenario, the relationship is built, but not established firmly nor does it have unrestricted access to the wonderful resources of heaven. It is a house of cards built on sand. On the outside, it looks like you have something real, but inwardly, it is hollow and shaky. One strong wind can take it out and will in a matter of time. This child (relationship) was conceived, birthed, and grown from the earth only. It is earthly and can never enter the Kingdom of God in that state. It MUST be born again from above. This is what it looks like to build using earthly wisdom, instead of wisdom from the Lord.

This is not the wisdom that comes down from above, but is earthly, unspiritual, demonic. For where jealousy and selfish ambition exist, there will be disorder and every vile practice. But the wisdom from above is first pure, then peaceable, gentle, open to reason, full of mercy and good fruits, impartial and sincere. And a harvest of righteousness is sown in peace by those who make peace.
James 3:15-18

Creating from the second realm (the created, unseen heavenly realm):
You are on the earth and have an offense against someone. You think, "If I can communicate how they made me feel and the wrong they caused, perhaps they will be moved with compassion or guilt and apologize to me. Then, I will feel better, and we can move forward.

But wisely, you understand that everything has a spiritual component- you know that you won't win this battle alone: you know you must go higher.

So, you head up to the heavenly realm (second realm where demons, angels and subatomic particles exist) and start praying, meditating, burning sage, making confessions, setting intentions, asking people to agree with you for things to go your way, reading tarot cards for knowledge, saying positive affirmations, wearing crystals, creating vision boards, requesting prayers from everyone you know on Facebook, visualizing a successful outcome, feeling the feelings, seeking prophets, seeking psychics, or maybe even casting spells for your desired outcome. (These are some of the many ways to manifest your desires on Earth. And yes, they often work if you hold it long enough, and with enough faith in the process. But watch what happens...)

Fully equipped with something conceived in the created heavenlies, you confront the person in great faith that it will go as you desire.

As you plead your case to the person, they hear you out, and are convinced

36

that you are right- it was their fault. They apologize and make peace with you, especially since you seem so spiritually superior to them. You must know something they don't. They are weighing in their minds the pros and cons of reconciling with you (tree of good and evil), and they have decided the good of your relationship outweighs the bad.

Things went your way- you have conceived and birthed a child from the second realm through the laws of attraction, vibration, and manifestation. But the frequency of that vibration is a lower-level, temporal tone, and on that frequency is every equal and matching desire: "good for me is more important than good for we". (I just made that expression up on the spot. Haha- that's a good one.) On this frequency, no one truly wins. You both have taken from the tree of the knowledge of good and evil, not knowing the fruit from that tree always results in eventual death. It's a law. As above, so below.

Alternately, they too are spiritual, and can see the dichotomy of your desires versus their desires, and they refuse to bend the knee to you. They can see in the spirit that your paths no longer intertwine, and they walk on, both injured and irritated that you tried to dominate them with your spiritual power.

They know what you know and hope someone humbles you along the path. No one won.

Now, let's look at what it could look like to create from the third realm, the eternal realm of the Kingdom of God:

You are on the earth and have an offense against someone. You think, "If I can communicate how they made me feel and the wrong they caused, perhaps they will be moved with compassion or guilt and apologize to me. Then, I will feel better, and we can move forward.

By wisdom, you are aware that everything is created in the spirit before you see it in the flesh, so you take the matter higher. But you also know, the second realm is just the womb of creation- you need more than a womb for this matter because you don't want to just birth any sort of relationship. You want to birth something good, pleasing, and perfect, straight from the Father of Lights. You know that with those gifts, there are no shadows or "pros and cons". You don't want to birth another "Ishmael." You only want wins for all because you are a smart person who doesn't like wasting time on stuff that's not for you.

Don't worry about anything, but in everything, through prayer and
petition with thanksgiving, let your requests be made known to God.
And the peace of God, which surpasses every thought, will guard your
hearts and minds in Christ Jesus.
Finally brothers, whatever is true, whatever is honorable, whatever is
just, whatever is pure, whatever is lovely, whatever is commendable—if
there is any moral excellence and if there is any praise—dwell on these
things.
Philippians 4:6-8

So, you get in a quiet place, perhaps with peaceful surroundings, and you silence every voice in your head, knowing that when the voices stop, you will

be able to hear the ever-present, always speaking, perfect voice of God.

As you wait, a voice pops up: "What they did was wrong. You have the right to confront them- they need to be held accountable."

Your soul starts to get agitated as you begin remembering what they did. With your weapon of mass destruction, your mind composes the most eloquent letter of accusation to the offender. You are confident that this will set the record straight and humble them to contrition.

Then in the waaaaay back of the room of your mind, you hear a tiny voice that says, "you did that once, too. I gave you mercy and no one ever knew you did it."

Ugg. You know it's true, so you silence their accuser.

Again, another voice says, "If you do not put an end to this behavior, they will continue to go down a path of destruction, and their blood will be on your hands. You MUST do something."

A little closer now, you hear that tiny voice saying, "The hearts of kings are like channels of water in my hands- I turn them any way I choose."

You understand that God is the only one who can compel their hearts to change, and that "Holy Spirit" is not one of the job descriptions on your resume.

Over and over, these sorts of conversations progress in that quiet moment, until finally, you hear the One True God speak loud and clear:

"Do you love me? Feed my sheep."

You ask, "How, Father?"

He replies: "Humble yourself before the mighty hand of God. Submit to me. Resist the devil and he will flee. You are my child. They are my child. I love you both and know your hearts. I know the plans I have for both of you. Separately, according to my purposes, and it is GOOD. Pray for them, and pray for yourself, to know me and to know my ways. I have good for all. I have given you the Mind of Christ, and you are free to access it in every moment of your life. I even speak to you in your dreams, as you sleep. I will guide you and lead you into all truth if you will let me. And I will do the same for them if they will let me. I force no human to bend to my will. You are given free will to do as you please on earth. It is my will for you to make Earth look exactly like my abode- the Kingdom of God. My culture should infiltrate the entire globe. My light and truth should govern the days and nights of the sphere. The heavens belong to me, but I have given YOU ALL the earth to rule over. If there are issues on the earth, you are my managers- solve the problems according to the ordinances and resources I have freely given to you. As above, so below. On Earth as it is in Heaven. It is my will for all to prosper and for all to come to the saving knowledge of truth. In this way, salvation is for Earth as it is in Heaven. And you will accomplish all of this through love, not as the world gives love (conditional, narcissistic, demanding, self-serving, strings attached, emotion-driven), but as I give love.

Love is the governor of truth. And truth is the governor of freedom.

Love them my way, not your way- you do not know the way on your own. This will shine light into the dark places of their hearts and yours. Then the truth will be clearly seen, and when they receive truth, they will be totally, completely free. And you receive truth, you will be totally, completely free. This is why Jesus came: as love that shines light that overcomes darkness, reveals the truth, and sets captives free. In this way, you will win. And they will win, too. This is the Kingdom of God: on Earth as it is in Heaven. Now, child: go and manage this situation unto the freedom of both of you. YOU are my governors on earth. These are your problems to manage. I have given you everything you need for life and godliness. Do not fear- I am with you. Govern with my love."

And there, you are humbled, and understand this situation isn't about you. And it's not about them, either. It's always about the perfect will of God known and performed on the earth, just as it is in heaven, because it brings glory to God, and righteousness, peace and JOY to you and everyone who partakes of your gifts and offerings. Prosperity is for all.

You understand that today, in this moment, you can bring the culture of the Kingdom into this broken relationship, knowing that the other person has the ability to choose whichever outcome they desire. You know that as you sit next to Christ in the third realm, you look to your right, and you see the person you are interceding for, next to you, next to Christ, next to God the Father, you all are looking below your feet into the second realm, the churning, energized, electric, protoplasmic womb of creation, with great expectation of a conceiving a beautiful, powerful life-giving child of promise in the form of good for each person, and for all. Then you see below that, the earthly realm, and every one of your enemies crushed under all your feet - hatred, bitterness, rage, jealousy, lust, murder, idolatry, sexual perversion, poverty, disease, mental illness, and every imaginable demonic dark force under heaven- they are looking up, with their hands trying to hold up the sky above them. But as you sit on the thrones in the Kingdom, you press the firmament below harder until they are destroyed. And you understand that whether your person reconciles with you or not, or whether you should continue in relationship with them or not, your newly understood approach to peace will be the exact seed that is needed to produce the child of righteousness that God desires to be born on the earth. You are at peace with knowing that ultimately, the person WILL walk in righteousness with God, fulfilling their own calling on the planet, whether that includes you or not. And so will you, with or without them intertwined. You have peace with that because you know God is faithful and He WILL perform what He promises. You lay down all your own desires and will, and let the Lord fill you with HIS desires, energizing your spirit with WHY you exist, renewing your soul to His truth, giving your body instructions on WHAT to do and HOW to do it on Earth…as it is already finished in Heaven.

It's clear to you now: By wisdom, you build the house- you know what needs to be done. By understanding of the womb of creation and how to birth children into freedom instead of slavery to your own desires, its foundation is firm and solid: established by God himself. And By knowledge, every resource you need to fill the house flows down from the throne of the Kingdom of God, flooding the house with kindness, love, financial provision, fidelity, truth, justice, healing and health, mental, physical, spiritual and sexual wholeness, faithfulness, God ideas, transportation, fun vacations, peace, joy, beautiful homes, jewelry, patience, unique skills and talents, fun cars, favor, spouses, and children…the list is unlimited. Every good gift that you can think of flows freely from God.

And you see clearly, if it does not get seeded from the third realm and then conceived and carried in the second realm, finally birthed into the first realm, you don't want it. It will come with shadows, and you will pay, and others will, too, resulting in trauma and death.

With that, you know exactly what to do, and you take action, knowing that no matter what, the person you are interceding for WILL prosper. And so will you. Together or separately: it matters not. God knows what is best,

41

and He will perform His will for each of you as you allow Him. All is well.

This is what Jesus meant when He said, "You must be born again, of the Spirit and water." Remember in Genesis where the Spirit of God hovered over the waters as He was preparing to birth the world and all it contains?

The Spirit of God exists in the eternal Kingdom realm and is the seed of all His creation. Defined as "life" or "breath of God", the seed of the Holy Spirit is implanted into the second realm- the created unseen womb of creation. It is described as water and contains all creative matter- it is the quantum realm where things unseen become matter. Through the Spirit AND water, His new life is born into the world for all to see and experience.

"By faith, we understand that the universe was created by God's command, so that what is seen was made out of what is invisible."
Hebrews 11:3

From eternity, He spoke into the womb of the second realm: "Be." And it was so: seen on earth. All three realms engaged.

In terms of salvation, the concept is the same:

In the earthly realm, a man and a woman come together. His earthly seed is implanted into her watery womb, and a child is conceived and manifested. When fully birthed, it is a child of the earth. Its soul was manifested in the second realm, and its flesh is seen in the first realm. Its spirit is considered "carnal"- of the created seen and unseen world (first and second realm). As the child grows, it sets its mind on things of the flesh: its soul desires and craves, and the child takes action to acquire what it wants for its flesh. It throws fits, cries, takes from others, hits, lies, cheats, and steals, and won't give back. In its natural, earthly form, its soul is protecting its flesh. Self-preservation is the most important thing to a child. Every response is born from the first and second realms.

It was "born this way"-carnal, desiring things that soothe its flesh.
We are all born this way.

But as it grows, he begins to sense that there may be more to life than taking for self. The child will give and get rewarded for it. The good feeling that comes with appreciation and gratitude from others becomes a seed in the soul (second realm, womb of creation). After a few more attempts at giving, and the reward that follows, the seed is allowed to sprout and grow, creating a paradigm that testifies to the product of goodness. The child wants more, and the existential search is awakened.

If the child seeks to give and share and produce good things on the earth from the first realm only, he will receive based on the most powerful law of that realm: The Law of Sowing and Reaping. Whatever he does to others, it will come back to him in varying amounts, depending on the quality of the seed and the soil it was grown in. Give and take. What he receives is in direct proportion to what he gives, based on his own good (or evil) works in the flesh, on earth. If the soil he sows in is good (people or things), and his seed is good, he will receive good in return. If the soil he sows in is bad (a bad investment or sown into a person or thing that does not value the seed), his return will be minimal, if any- the soil doesn't have the nourishment to cause the seed to grow. If his seed is bad, but the soil is good, he will still receive nothing, because the seed is dead. (In this realm, we get out what we put in.)

In this way, he will operate according to the economy of the earth, and yield to its laws, as limiting as they are. This is called "The Law of Sin and Death": You break a law of the earth, death follows. No mercy. Only consequences of actions, good or evil.

Don't be deceived: God is not mocked. For whatever a man sows he will also reap, because the one who sows to his flesh will reap corruption from the flesh, but the one who sows to the Spirit will reap eternal life from the Spirit.
Galatians 6:7-8

If the child seeks to give and share and produce good things on earth from the second realm into the first realm, he will receive based on the higher laws of vibration. Just as the Law of Lift defies the Law of Gravity, so the Law of Vibration supersedes the Law of Sowing and Reaping. He will have sort of spiritual awakening that allows him to recognize his own spiritual side and want to explore creating in that realm. He will understand that as a man thinks in his heart (soul, second realm), so he is. He may meditate or pray or visualize or use those tools I mentioned earlier that allow manifestations to flow down to the first realm, and it will start to work for him. He may begin to understand the power of heart-mind coherence and see that when his thoughts are in harmony with his emotions, he will glide effortlessly on the vibration of that frequency, for good or evil. As he harnesses his abilities, he will see results, but he will also understand the laws are completely dependent upon his own ability to work with the laws. He is the driver of success or failure according to his understanding of spiritual laws, and he is the architect, builder, and keeper of the world he created. He will understand the laws of sowing and reaping, but he will understand the laws of vibration are higher laws than sowing and reaping. Because if he can master his mind and emotions, he can move mountains with a word. For good or evil.

The two key issues with operating in this way are:

First: The laws of vibration are so powerful that when harnessed, it allows a person to create almost anything he sets his mind to. Where intention is bad, the created thing is evil. Some of the most evil minds in history understood these laws and worked with them to create the world they wanted to live in. It is said that the power Hitler possessed was created in this manner. In 1918, a psychologist named Edmond Foster treated soldier, Adolf Hitler for hysterical blindness. He hypnotized Hitler, leading him to believe that though miracles have ceased to exist for most people, he was superior and was created to fulfill a superior purpose on earth. Under hypnosis, he explained to Hitler that for that reason, he could receive healing of sight if his will were strong enough. In that moment, Hitler agreed, was cured, and went on to believe the vision spoken over his life. Because he mastered the art and science of working with the laws of vibration and applied faith, he was able to mark history indelibly, forever. (Hitler called it the "Triumph of the Will".) Because his heart was evil and full of murderous intent, he was able to use his understanding of power in the second realm to annihilate millions from the planet, including the hypnotist who "cured" him. Angels AND demons operate in this realm, and the one you work with shows up according to whose will you want to enact: your own or the Lord's. The Lord's angels ONLY take flight at the voice of God's commands- they work with us only when we say what God says, or if God Himself commands them. *(Psalm 103:20-21; Hebrews 1: 13-14)* Demons enact the will of the enemy, according to your flesh. Speak your own desires, and they'll help you get your own will accomplished. But then they'll kill you, too, because you are not their master: Satan is. Look at Hitler. His end was not glorious.

Witches and spiritualists beware: The god of that power desires to take you out, too. And will. People may say that God took Hitler out as an act of justice, but really, the enemy had the authority to take him because Hitler operated under the Law of Sin and Death in the first two realms: the cost for sin is death. Remember the James 1:15 scripture that said, "when sin is fully grown, it results in death"? The original translation says, "when sin is accomplished in you, then you die." Satan had his way with Hitler. And then he was done with him. (I'm thinking also, he finished with him once Hitler got sick in his mind and body- both of which were put on him by Satan. He couldn't use Hitler's body anymore, so he was done with him.)

As unfair as it seems to us, if Hitler would have put himself under the Law of the Spirit of Life in Christ Jesus, he too could have been granted mercy from the Father. Dead seeds can be resurrected to life under this law (in the third realm). This is hard to understand for us, but it involves repentance, being born again, and receiving a renewed mind, resulting in a life of Godliness. This is what happened to Paul in the New Testament.

Therefore, no condemnation now exists for those in Christ Jesus, because the Spirit's law of life in Christ Jesus has set you free from the law of sin and of death. What the law could not do since it was

45

limited by the flesh, God did.
(Romans 8:1-2)

God is faithful.

Note, being under the Law of the Spirit of Life means that you are operating on earth from the third realm. That means you are doing the Will of GOD on earth, not your own. Jesus said, "whoever does the will of the Father God"- that's who belongs to Him. *(Matthew 7:21-23)*

God is not willing that any would perish, but that all would come to the saving knowledge of Christ. The thief comes to kill, steal, and destroy everyone. Jesus came that you would have life abundantly, in this realm, and eternally.

Secondly: The laws only work when you do. Operating in this realm requires iron will and a strong spirit. If at any point you stumble, the law will spit you out of the realm, down to earth. It can feel like it is you versus the world. Entrepreneurs talk often about how lonely it is on their journey. This is because they know they must stay in the second realm to succeed, and it requires extreme focus and concentration in the mind to do so. I used to operate here when I first began my business. I could only last six years before it spat me out. When I jumped back in, a few years later, I had the knowledge to go higher... to The Kingdom, where my Father lives and loves to protect and provide every good thing for me...and you. And His mercy and grace endure forever, even when I faint. He covers all my weaknesses with His love and provision.

An important note about those first two realms: There is a spiritual veil that exists between the third realm and the second realm. It is "the door" into the Kingdom of Heaven, and the only way to pass through it is through Jesus Himself: He is the door. He tore down the veil when He finished His work on the cross.

When we operate from the first two realms instead of going through the veil into the third realm, we are taking from the tree of the knowledge of good and evil. We are weighing good and bad, pros and cons, and judging based on laws that were created by man within those realms. We put ourselves in the position as judge and jury over the earth, writing our own laws and moral codes, deciding what is right and wrong. We were never meant to rule this way: there is only one lawgiver and judge: the Maker and Keeper of everything. If you have ever been subject to injustice, or lived (or died) during 2020, you can easily understand why this is a problem. Remember those to whom you were in direct moral/political/social/medical/religious opposition during that year? Did you want them judging you and making laws for you? Me, neither.

What we know and understand about taking from that tree is that the fruit we create results in earthly death. That fruit is cannibalistic: it eats its own kind. A good example of what these results look like can be found in the journey to success. Many times, we see a person sacrifice everything held dear in order to achieve a financial goal in business. As observers, we watch in movies and in real life, how a person applies the earthly laws of success to gain the world. But as the scriptures say, "What does it profit a man to gain the world, but lose his soul?"

Alternately we've seen many sacrifice the temporary things of life for the greater good. We see them build up, consistently choosing others' welfare over their own comforts, and are richly rewarded by God for it, with love, protection, companionship, and provision. I've watched this play out in my parents' lives, and the enjoyment they have received on this earth now because of it. My mom always says, everything is for legacy. They gave up much, and shared everything they had with anyone who had need. As I was growing up, my mom and dad went many nights without dinner so that my cousins and siblings and I could eat. Now, they are able to share their beautiful lakehouse, and all they own with us all; They've created a place of peace and respite for their legacy.

In the end, everything we create on earth will be put to fire and burn. Anything created outside of the third realm will not remain. Because flesh and blood will not enter the Kingdom (*1 Corinthians 15:50*).

If it wasn't born from above, from the Will of God, it is not eternal.

I talk to my kids often about our power as humans to manifest the things we desire from realm to realm. I always tell them that even without the knowledge of the third realm, we still have the ability to make things come to life. The principles of manifesting are inherent in our DNA: God made us in His image, with the ability to create the world we want to live in- we are co-creators with Elohim.

But when we create on our own, outside of the will of God and the third realm, we are prone to creating selfishly, with ideas that may seem great at the time, but once born and observed, can ruin lives. That is exactly what the slave child from my dream is: born from selfish desires. Its end is always death, and someone (or many) always suffers.

What is born of flesh is flesh. What is born of The Spirit is spirit. -John 3:6

But now, I will show you a better way.

Journal Entry
Witches Everywhere.
The church has stifled the knowledge of the Power of God in His Children
for more than 16 centuries out of fear, ignorance, and control.
Because of it, witches are becoming mainstream.
Not because of their desire for godlessness, but rather because their divine nature testifies to their souls that they have the Power of God in them,
and they want to use it to create a world they want to live in.
But since the church isn't leading this training,
people are turning to earthly (1st and 2nd realm) resources.
And as it goes, when we look to the CREATED things for power,
instead of the CREATOR of all things, who is forever to be praised,

the truth gets distorted, and the counterfeit comes.
Our good intentions turn sour as we try to balance "good versus evil"
- the fruit from that famous tree in the garden.
We find ourselves entangled in GREAT DARKNESS. AND DEATH
FOLLOWS. (Romans 1)

We were never meant to partake of THAT TREE.
Life only.
Pray for the witches to take from the tree of Life only: the fruit of the
Creator.
They are seeking truth and the Power of God in them.
They just don't know the source yet.
As they figure it out, they will do the works of God that
a great many of "Christians" are too passive to do.
"All of creation is groaning in travail, waiting for the children of God to
step up".
The witches are trying to step up. Believers need to usher them in with
Truth.
They are willing to do the work.
And pray for yourself, too.
Witches aren't the only ones who do this.
Win-lose mindset: if someone must lose so you can win- That is NOT
the gospel.
That, too, is witchcraft.
Life is for ALL.
But the message of Christ IN us has been watered down to a
gospel that only speaks to suffering on this earth to inherit eternal peace.
That is NOT the Gospel that Jesus spoke or lived out,
but that is the message many are living with today.
The harvest is plenty, but the workers are few. Jesus didn't say pray for
the lost sheep.
In that context, He said pray for the workers.
Too many of God's children don't want to do the work.

Step up, Christians. Take your positions.
Feed His sheep.
Love them.
Love the lost ones.
Don't Lose One.

———————————-

I have been attracting a LOT of witches lately.
I'm assuming it's partly because of my hair and my profession-
they are calling me an alchemist- I'm ok with that. (I work with plants
in cosmetics).
But I also know they are drawn to me because they are sensing that I
operate in my divine nature in the spirit realm.
I operate in the Power of God in me, as His daughter... as a King of the
Earth.
I am learning how to operate as Jesus did:
Calling things into existence, manifesting what has freely been given to
me through Christ, healing the sick, raising the dead, casting off
demons, setting people free.
I privately want to walk on water and translate in time. Jesus did,
as did many in the Bible. And He said we could too- and even greater
things,
because of the power of the Holy Spirit in us.
I suspect I will do it if it is needed- not just for fun. I want to do it, even
for fun-
but God knows I'll tell everyone. I always tell the fun stuff.
He doesn't want us enamored with the miracle. He wants us enamored
with Him.
I'm enamored with Him.
He never once said, "Don't try this at home, folks. I'm God- you can't
do it."
In fact, when Peter asked to walk on water, Jesus said, "Ok. Come."
Peter did it and only sank when he stopped believing.
Jesus did not do those things because He was God;

He was able to do them because of the fullness of the Holy Spirit in Him.
He was so full of the Spirit that he said, "Satan has nothing in me."
Satan couldn't hold Him back because He was totally,
completely surrendered to the Will of God.
That's how we can do things too:
First a little, and then more, as we surrender our own will.
Our prayers look less like: "Lord, please let me have favor to get that job",
and more like: "Lord, I thank you that you guide me and lead me to do YOUR work, wherever that is, and your favor surrounds me like a shield.
I go where you say go, and I stay where you say stay."
In this place of surrender, we move mountains and walk on water and pull money from fishes' mouths and raise the dead. Jesus said we should. And could. If we believe.

We are ALL Alchemists, created to Co-Create with the Living God.
The Universe and Nature were created to bend the knee to the Will of God.
And as He is, so are we in this world. They yield to us.
The creature is never greater that the creator.

Our role in this colonization of heaven on earth as co-creators with God is meant to bring Glory to the King, life to those we serve, and to make us very happy.
On Earth, as it is already done in Heaven. Jesus said to do it. WE do it on Earth.
He already did it in Heaven.
We manifest it down.
Everything I've said is found in the Word of God.
I'm always HAPPY to give the scriptures. Just ask. Or google it yourself. It's there on your phone.

———————————————————-

Last year, I was in a restaurant with friends.
A man and his wife came to me and told me how much they liked my hair.
The woman started petting my hair (a LOT) and kept remarking how much she was drawn to it.
She said, "it's like a powerful witch's hair."
I smiled and said to her, "No- it's MORE powerful than a witch's hair- it's the Glory of God on me."
She was taken aback a bit, and her husband said, "but this has power"- and he held up the crystal around his neck.
I said, "that crystal was created by God to emit energy- it is not the source of energy, but only a physical conduit of it. God is the maker and keeper of it.
The created thing is never more powerful than the CREATOR."

Crystals serve us. We do not serve them. The earth MUST yield to us.

He also was taken aback, but they both nodded their heads.
I blessed them in Christ and the woman hugged me.
Then my sister said, "why does that crap always happen to you?!?"
She only saw the woman petting me.
But she's right- it always happens to me because I have yielded my will to God and will share truth to anyone He sends my way. I often attract scenes like that in public.
I used to hate it, but I'm learning not to be embarrassed anymore.

"The Spirit of the Living God is upon me, and He has anointed me to preach the Gospel of the good news to the poor, give sight to the blind, set the captive free, and to proclaim the year of the FAVOR of God."
It's on YOU, too. If you want it.
And the best part: we don't even have to be weird about it.
Jesus hung out with the "sinners" but brought them into light with the truth.

The religious rulers were pissed because He was getting results with light and truth of who HE was as a true son.
He set people free from their ungodly desires and gave them power, but the religious remained bound by choice.
Set them free.
Set yourself free.

7

The Good News of the Gospel of Peace

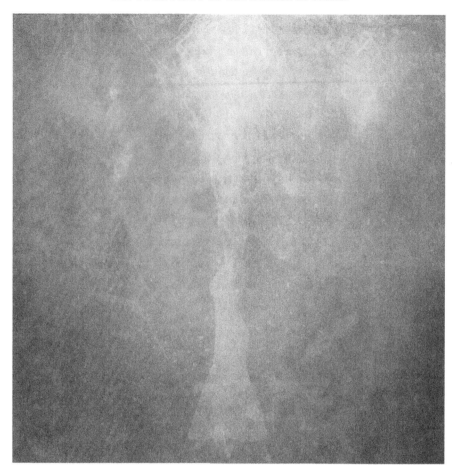

"Revival"

I was waiting for you.
I knew you would come.

For a child will be born for us,
a son will be given to us,
and the government will be on His shoulders.
He will be named
Wonderful Counselor, Mighty God,
Eternal Father, Prince of Peace.
The dominion will be vast,
and its prosperity will never end.
He will reign on the throne of David
and over his kingdom,
to establish and sustain it
with justice and righteousness from now on and forever.
The zeal of the Lord of Hosts will accomplish this.
Isaiah 9: 6-7

I t was never a religion.

It was always a government.

Welcome to the Kingdom of God. On earth, as it is in Heaven. I felt a leap in my spirit as I wrote this.

Let's return to the newborn child made by a man and a woman. We remember in Genesis where the Spirit of God hovered over the waters as He was preparing to birth the world and all it contains. We saw that God was in the third realm, creating/ conceiving into the watery womb of the second realm and manifesting the produce into the first realm.

That's how God Himself created. As He is, so are we in this world.

Now look:

Jesus replied, "I assure you: Unless someone is born again, he cannot see
the kingdom of God."
"But how can anyone be born when he is old?" Nicodemus asked Him.
"Can he enter his mother's womb a second time and be born?"
Jesus answered, "I assure you: Unless someone is born of water and the

Spirit, he cannot enter the kingdom of God. Whatever is born of the flesh is flesh, and whatever is born of the Spirit is spirit. Do not be amazed that I told you that you must be born again. The wind blows where it pleases, and you hear its sound, but you don't know where it comes from or where it is going. So it is with everyone born of the Spirit."
John 3: 3-8

Notice Jesus said, "whatever is born of flesh is flesh. Whatever is born of the (Holy) Spirit is spirit." The second realm is spiritual and contains demons and angels and spiritual things. But it is not the home of the Holy Spirit, nor is it eternal. Spiritual and Holy Spirit are not the same. And I promise you: they do not "lock horns", as one of my favorite teachers says. They are not evenly matched. Holy Spirit is the supreme power of God at work in us-God's "dunamis" power...His dynamic power. Like dynamite. It is the same power God used to create the worlds. Nothing compares to this power, and nothing can compete with it. The Bible says Jesus used the finger of God to flick off demons. No problem at all. We can, too, when we do it from the third realm.

Dunamis:

1. Strength, Power, Ability
2. Inherent Power, Power Residing in A Thing by Virtue Of Its Nature, Or Which A Person Or Thing Exerts And Puts Forth
3. Power For Performing Miracles
4. Moral Power and Excellence of Soul
5. The Power and Influence Which Belong to Riches And Wealth
6. Power And Resources Arising in Numbers
7. Power Consisting In or Resting Upon Armies, Forces, Hosts

And the same dunamis, Holy Spirit power that raised Christ from the dead (along with all of us!) lives in those who have the Holy Spirit in them, giving the same dead-raising, sickness-healing, demon-casting, life-giving power to our mortal bodies. As He is, so are we in this world.

As. He. Is. So. Are. We. In. This. World.

If we could genuinely believe that, even a fraction as much as Hitler believed the vision spoken over his life, we would transform the globe in a matter of minutes. This thing would be over, and we all would be walking gloriously in Kingdom bliss, all together, forever. Because remember my dream, and the military "V" pattern we moved into for ease and speed? Imagine how quickly we could turn this world around if even two percent of the population believed they were who God said they were, and acted accordingly...

So, if nothing born of the flesh can experience the Kingdom of God on Earth, and if you must be born again to be "born of the Spirit," how exactly can we be born again?

I'm glad you and Nicodemus asked.

Imagine yourself as a metaphorical (and metaphysical) seed that grows into a plant whose purpose is to produce good fruit on the planet and be the boss of it.

You are first produced by a man and a woman who become entangled in the flesh; together, his seed and her egg produce you: a human being.

Your soul and spirit enter the second realm, and your flesh enters the first realm.

You exist in those two realms until one day, your soul hears a word- a seed: The Word of the Living God- an incorruptible seed.

> *Do not say in your heart, "Who will go up to heaven?" that is, to bring*
> *Christ down or, "Who will go down into the abyss?" that is, to bring*
> *Christ up from the dead. On the contrary, what does it say? The*
> *message is near you, in your mouth and in your heart, this is the*
> *message of faith that we proclaim: If you confess with your mouth,*

58

"Jesus is Lord," and believe in your heart that God raised Him from the
dead, you will be saved. One believes with the heart, resulting in
righteousness, and one confesses with the mouth, resulting in salvation.
For everyone who calls on the name of the Lord will be saved.
Romans 10:6-13

When your soul and flesh receive that seed, the Word, it begins the process of death and rebirth.

Just like every seed, how does a seed become a plant?

It gets planted into the ground and dies.

""I assure you: Unless a grain of wheat falls to the ground and dies, it
remains by itself. But if it dies, it produces a large crop.
John 12:24

Your mind, will, emotions, desires, ego, and flesh are surrendered to the will of God. You understand that nothing you could do on your own could ever amount to the beauty and power of what God can do through you. You want everything He wants for you. Nothing more. Nothing less. You lay your life down.

Then, something wonderful happens: from the third realm, the Spirit of God himself hovers over the dark watery depths of the second realm, dropping your spiritual seed into that realm, and once more, you are born again.

Only this time, you are born from above: spirit, soul, and body. You are born again of water and The Spirit.

Jesus is the way, the truth, and the life. No one comes to the Father in the third realm except through the Son. By Him and through Him, you have entered the Kingdom with God. *(John 14:6)*

Be at rest: you are home.

And now, you are seated in the third realm with Christ, who is your co-heir to everything that was made, filled with His **knowledge**, and together you create the world you want to live in, according to the perfect will of God for everyone. Together you look down upon the second and first realms, **understanding** what needs to be done, and tell your body, which is hanging out on earth, to make it happen through **wisdom**.

Can you see it now?

This is why Jesus came to the earth: to reunite us with our Creator and His divine purpose for us on the earth: to make the colony of earth look just like heaven. As above, so below.

> *This is how we know that we remain in Him and He in us: He has given assurance to us from His Spirit. And we have seen, and we testify that the Father has sent His Son as the world's Savior. Whoever confesses that Jesus is the Son of God—God remains in him and he in God. And we have come to know and to believe the love that God has for us. God is love, and the one who remains in love remains in God, and God remains in him.*
>
> *In this, love is perfected with us so that we may have confidence in the day of judgment, **for we are as He is in this world**. There is no fear in love; instead, perfect love drives out fear, because fear involves punishment. So the one who fears has not reached perfection in love. We love because He first loved us.*
> 1 John 4: 13-19

The Creative Power of Subatomic Faith

We understand through the study of quantum science that the subatomic realm is the storehouse of creative matter, and waves and particles are the microscopic systems that create matter. But did you know that one system can exist in two places at the same time? I'm not saying it is a wave/particle that split in two; I'm saying it's the same wave/particle in two places at once. It's called "quantum superposition of a function." If you've heard of the "Schrödinger's Cat" experiment, you can understand: When an electron is in superposition of function, it is in two states at once, one spinning in one direction and the other spinning in the opposite direction. Its goal and end is to collapse into a singular possibility...to choose to become a thing. And the strangest part of it all is that only when the system is "measured" does it collapse into an observable position. And what is the system of measurement? Human interpretation, and frequent interaction with the environment of the system.

The human mind is the tool of measurement!

The system must be focused on to become. First, it has to be seen and decided upon in the mind of the observer. Then, the function obeys the vision and becomes what the observer saw in the mind. The observer is the deciding factor in its collapsed position. The observer decides what it will become. There's an expression that says, "what you think about, you bring about." This is the science to that ideology. God agrees.

Take every thought captive to the obedience of Christ and punish every disobedient thought. (2 Corinthians 10:5)

Why would we need to punish disobedient thoughts if they were benign? I love the quotation from James Allen in the book, *As A Man Thinketh (Allen, 1903):*

Mind is the master power that molds and makes,
And man is mind, and evermore he takes
The tool of thought, and, shaping what he wills,
brings forth a thousand joys, a thousand ills-
He thinks in secret, and it comes to pass:
Environment is but his looking-glass.

I love how he calls the environment our looking glass. Because it's true: as you see in a moment how quantum entanglement and decoherence function, you'll recognize how critical it is for each person to cause his environment to yield to him.

You will see: either you create the environment, or the environment will create you.

We like to think that God is in control of our actions, but we are the ones who control our own minds and souls- it's all first and second-realm activity until we decide to enter into God's rest in the third realm. We decide to whom we will submit. And we take action accordingly. Our minds are the master power of our souls. Our soul tells our body what it is going to do. It can choose to submit its will to the Living God, or it can choose to go its own way. If this were not so, those Israelites would have crossed into the promised land in a few weeks. They chose to wrestle for forty years. The original exiles never entered into God's rest.

"The mind set on the flesh is death. But the mind set on the Spirit is life and peace." (Romans 8:6)

We set our minds and choose life or death.

And like Joshua and Caleb versus the spies they sent into Canaan (*Numbers 13*), the beauty and beast of that reality is: two people (observers) can look at the same subatomic matter (unseen possibility) and decide which way it will collapse for his own observation. That means, two or thousands or millions of observers can look at the same situation. One sees the possibility of good coming, and others see the possibility (probability) of bad coming. And for each observer, it will be unto them as they decide. God said so.

The LORD responded to Moses, "I have pardoned them as you requested. Yet as surely as I live and as the whole earth is filled with the LORD's glory, none of the men who have seen My glory and the signs I

performed in Egypt and in the wilderness, and have tested Me these 10
times and did not obey Me, will ever see the land I swore to give their
fathers. None of those who have despised Me will see it. But since My
servant Caleb has a different spirit and has followed Me completely, I
will bring him into the land where he has gone, and his descendants will
inherit it. Then the LORD spoke to Moses and Aaron: "How long must
I endure this evil community that keeps complaining about Me? I have
heard the Israelites' complaints that they make against Me. Tell them:
As surely as I live," this is the LORD's declaration, "I will do to you
exactly as I heard you say.
Numbers 14: 21-28

We think it. Then we feel it. Then it flows out of our mouths. Then we hold
it in our hands. For life or death. Just like God did, in the beginning of all
creation.

Think it. Feel it. Speak it. Hold it.

Think it. Feel it. Speak it. Hold it.

For life or death.

Jesus said, "I tell you that on the day of judgment, people will have to
account for every careless word they speak. For by your words, you will
be acquitted, and by your words you will be condemned." (Matthew
12:36-37)

"Of course that would happen! God is good!" versus, "Of course that would
happen! As usual, nothing goes right for me."

From the fruit of his mouth a man's stomach is satisfied;
he is filled with the product of his lips.
Life and death are in the power of the tongue,

and those who love it will eat its fruit.
Proverbs 18:21

Blessings and curses are laid before you: Life and death. YOU CHOOSE LIFE. So that you will live and your children's children also. Others won't choose life in the exact same situation. But YOU can. Joshua said, "As for me and MY house, WE WILL serve the Lord." (Joshua 24:15)

The Bible says speaks about superposition, too: in Christ, you are on earth in the flesh, and your spirit is in eternity with Christ. At the same time...now. Always. If you are not in Christ, or if you are in Him, but have allowed your mind to be distracted by the cares of the world (decoherence), your body is on the earth, and your spirit is in the second, spiritual realm, powerful, but not nearly as powerful and peaceful as we were made to be in the third realm. Hanging out in the second realm makes you susceptible to demonic influence also- because without the mind of Christ in the third realm, every spiritual thing looks good. It all looks powerful. And without the prepayment of Christ, it all has a price.

Science is catching up quickly with the Bible. As I've begun studying quantum mechanics, I have found scriptures to back up the discoveries easily, and I have no physics background. The same goes for the Laws of Vibration and the studies of neuroscience and the power of the mind. The caution is always: unless the Lord builds the house, those who build it labor in vain. It will collapse and great will be its destruction. Look around for examples like the ones I have given; You'll understand what I mean.

Did you also know the Bible says that we will judge the angels? *(1 Corinthians 6:3)* Angels and demons (fallen angels) exist in the second realm. When we are in Christ, we are seated above them all, and we will judge them all because they were sent to help US on earth. If they don't do their jobs, in the end of this age, they will be judged for it by us. That's how much authority we have as co-heirs with Christ, and how important it is for us all to finish the work we were put on the earth to accomplish. Let's do it.

Now we move here: Born Again. Of The Spirit. When you are born again, you officially inherit the Kingdom and all it contains.

8

Don't Be Drunk and Half-Asleep

"Esperanza"

*...and there remained this hope that one day,
she would fly.
Life had taught her,
you become the stories you tell yourself.
So with every breath,
she leaned forward
and with every dream,
she leaned in expectantly...
Flutter, flutter, fly...*

Esperanza high!

"Be alert and of sober mind. Your enemy the devil prowls around like a roaring lion looking for someone to devour. Resist him, standing firm in the faith..."
1 Peter 5:8

I hadn't paid attention to the strategies the slave woman used to attack my daughter when I originally had the dream. But now as I reinvestigate the dream, I realize that there were two tactics: one was to make her 'sleepy,' or unaware of the attack, and the other was to enchant her with golden shimmery glitter (ignore the fact that it wasn't shimmery at all to me- all I saw was dirt and dust).

When we are sober and awake, it's quite easy to spot dusty, dirty threats headed our way. In fact, sometimes it can be so obvious that it's comical. I remember when my daughter was a toddler, she would hide behind the sheer curtains to try to scare us. But as she stood watching us, eyes wide open, lips in full grin, we watched her right back, knowing that she thought she was about to give us a big shock. We could see everything clearly- her body, her position, her gaze, and her intent to scare. It was adorable, hilarious, and so much fun.

Demons can be like that sometimes, too- as they look at you, you're looking right back at them, knowing their intention and strategy and inability to get that one past you. Your response sounds something like, "are you being serious right now? Get out of here." and with that and an eye roll, the threat is dismissed. Sometimes it's that easy.

But other times, you get sideswiped by a demonic 18-wheeler and sent into a tailspin until your orientation is completely distorted and you can't remember who you were before the hit.

This is the type of attack we need to prepare for.

The way we prepare is to understand WHO we are, WHO advocates for us, and HOW a trial works in the court of the Kingdom.

Let's go back to the dream:

As a true child of the "Free woman", I knew that whatever was born in the back of that room was NOT my sibling, and it was NOT even an actual child. I knew that thing was not connected to me in any way, and I knew that the fake mother had NO power over my own daughter while I was there to protect her.

I understood my power to cause all of it to come to an end immediately. From the beginning of the dream, as the lies began, with my mom being confused about the provenance of the slave child, to the nurse and slave woman trying to convince me that they had power over me, and ending with the slave woman attempting to lure my daughter to its trap, I went in knowing I was going to shut it all down.

I knew it because I knew I could.

I knew I could because I had done it before.

And I could because I was given power and authority to do so. Authority was given to me by being a child of the true mother, in her house, whose house was my own. Power was given to me through confidence in my position as a true child and was doubled down by the military crew that fell in behind me: my prayer partners.

I've heard it said many times regarding spiritual authority and power: authority is like what police possess- they have been given authority by the government to enforce the laws of the land. Power is what police carry, in the form of weapons and officer backup: if they cannot get compliance with their own authority, they can get it by calling for more enforcement. They get help.

I knew going into the house that I had weapons of mass destruction within me and a military backing me- my prayer partners. We were fully equipped with power and authority to investigate the situation and enact the laws of the land.

In real life, we are given authority by Christ, through His finished work on the cross, to enact the laws of the Kingdom: on earth as it is in Heaven. With God as our father, and co-heirs with Christ himself, everything He said we can do, we are supposed to do:

Heal the sick.

Raise the dead.

Cleanse the leper.

Cast out demons.

Preach the Good News to the poor.

In real life, we are given power by the Holy Spirit to ensure the job gets done. Luckily, this power isn't for a select few who are special. It's for anyone who receives it, and it comes as they receive Christ.

> Jesus said, "I assure you: The one who believes in Me will also do the works that I do. And he will do even greater works than these because I am going to the Father. Whatever you ask in My name, I will do it so that the Father may be glorified in the Son. If you ask Me anything in My name, I will do it."
>
> John 14:12-12

The Bible also says that we don't wage war the way the world does, with guns and bombs. But rather, we have spiritual weapons of mass destruction in the form of our MINDS: we shut every liar, thief, and murderer down with our thoughts of the Knowledge of God. It says we take the enemy thoughts captive, and we punish them. In this way, we have the ability to tear down those walls, the strongholds that get built up in our own minds that say we can't win, or it won't work, or evil always prevails, or victory is impossible...or it will always be this way...or you were born like that and will never be any different.

My husband (I love him so much) recently said this about a war we are currently waging (and winning):

> The enemy (slave woman) will lure a person into his lies, get them to participate, and keep it hidden in the dark for just long enough to build a stronghold in the person's mind, with experiences to support the fortress. Then, once the paradigm and habits are created, he exposes their sin to start a war with those they love. He knows strongholds are hard to tear down without the knowledge of God. They make excellent prison walls.

Aaron also said that in war and chaos, if you can't tell what the enemy's intention/motive is, look at the result, and know: that was the intent. War, chaos, and utter destruction: that's the intent of the destroyer. Mission accomplished.

I knew a girl in high school who would go to one person and tell them a friend called them a bad name. Then she would go to the friend and say the other person responded in kind. She would incite the two of them to confront each other, and then watch as they fought it out. She loved it. I ran into her a decade later at a college I worked at, and she was alone and miserable. She was still up to her tricks, but not effective because she had no influence.

Side note: To anyone reading this who is involved in the occult and its practices, including "white magic", or anyone who is struggling with a religious or political spirit like the Pharisees, know that Satan is the father of both ideologies, and he will not back you up once you are deeply immersed; he wants to watch you burn. There is a true Father for you who wants life for you. He will open the door for you at any time. Feel free to go to Him- it's NEVER too late; you are never too far from Him. He adores you and is watching for you to run to Him.

At this point, we are aware of who we are: children of the true lawgiver and judge. Born again of The Spirit of God, equipped with power and authority to stop and convict assailants, with creation's greatest attorney that ever lived, (who also HAPPENS to be your spiritual co-heir!), Jesus Christ Himself. We can't lose.

So we take the battle to the Highest Court: The Throne of God. Notice in my dream, after I sent the nurse away and told my military to worship the Lord, I went straight to the slave woman and began charging him with crimes against humanity. I listed them out and finished with a verdict of guilt. I commanded him to leave and to take the slave baby with him. And it was done.

In the eyes of the Lord, those who have been born again of The Spirit have received the power and authority of Christ to command creation to submit to the laws of God. We are co-creators of the earth, with the ability and commission to make Earth look just like Heaven. As above, so below. It's our job to do so.

But HOW do we know what heaven looks like, so that we can make earth share the same culture?

I pray that the God of our Lord Jesus Christ, the glorious Father, would give you a spirit of wisdom and revelation in the knowledge of Him. I pray that the perception of your mind may be enlightened so you may know what is the hope of His calling, what are the glorious riches of His inheritance among the saints, and what is the immeasurable greatness of His power to us who believe, according to the working of His vast strength.

He demonstrated this power in the Messiah by raising Him from the dead and seating Him at His right hand in the heavens— far above every ruler and authority, power and dominion, and every title given, not only in this age but also in the one to come. And He put everything under His feet and appointed Him as head over everything for the church, which is His body, the fullness of the One who fills all things in every way.

Together with Christ Jesus He also raised us up and seated us in the heavens, so that in the coming ages He might display the immeasurable riches of His grace through His kindness to us in Christ Jesus. For you are saved by grace through faith, and this is not from yourselves; it is God's gift— not from works, so that no one can boast. For we are His creation, created in Christ Jesus for good works, which God prepared ahead of time so that we should walk in them.

Ephesians 1: 17-23; 2: 4-10

We are His creation, created in Christ Jesus for good works, which God prepared ahead of time so that we should walk in them.

We are HIS creation.

Created in Christ for good works.

Which God prepared ahead of time.

So that we should walk in them.

Let that sink in for a moment. Every point.

This is WHY we are here.

Selah.

We were always God's first love. Our soul knows full well. Pause and worship with me now- He is so beautiful.
   Selah.
   We can know how to design the earth by two tools that have been freely given to us:

The Word of God and the Spirit of God.

Jesus said, "But an hour is coming, and is now here, when the true worshipers will worship the Father in spirit and truth. Yes, the Father wants such people to worship Him. God is spirit, and those who worship Him must worship in spirit and truth." (John 4:23, 24)
   The Word of God is the Living Will and Testament of God to His heirs. Everything we need to know about life and godliness is recorded in the will, once for all time. It can divide truth from lies and reveal the DNA blueprint for each person.

For the word of God is living and effective and sharper than any double-edged sword, penetrating as far as the separation of soul and spirit, joints and marrow. It is able to judge the ideas and thoughts of

the heart.
Hebrews 4:12

The Spirit of God lives inside every person who is born again, entangled with their spirit, and speaks constantly to anyone who has ears to hear. It's a beautiful thing to tune one's ear to the voice of Jesus- it's like tuning a radio to a particular frequency- as you turn the dial finely, the sound becomes clearer. In fact, we've always heard preachers and people say, "God's ways are mysterious... you just never know what He will do..."

But in the Word, it states it *used to be said*, "eyes haven't seen, ears haven't heard, nor have hearts understood all that God has planned", but now He has made know His plans to us through His Spirit.

In fact, it says we have the actual Mind of Christ. That means we can know whatever we need to know when we need to know it. (*1 Corinthians 2:8-16*)

When the Spirit of truth comes, He will guide you into all the truth. For He will not speak on His own, but He will speak whatever He hears. He will also declare to you what is to come. He will glorify Me, because He will take from what is Mine and declare it to you. Everything the Father has is Mine. This is why I told you that He takes from what is Mine and will declare it to you.
John 16:13-14

I know it sounds weird, but when I was a college student and hadn't prepared for a test, I would pray my way through the tests. It worked many times. I didn't know why it was working, but because it often worked, I often used it. Haha! I know it's not the best way to develop discipline, but God is faithful, and His mercy endures forever.

The Mind of Christ/ Spirit of Truth is our superpower, and when used with authority, will get us exactly what we were sent by God to get. Which in my opinion, is all I ever want. No more, no less.

When we understand our position on earth, we can put on our "Armor of God" with full confidence in our ability to get the job done successfully.

Then we become Weapons of Mass Destruction.

> For though we live in the body, we do not wage war in an unspiritual way, since the weapons of our warfare are not worldly, but are powerful through God for the demolition of strongholds. We demolish arguments and every high-minded thing that is raised up against the **knowledge of God**, taking every thought captive to obey Christ. And we are ready to punish any disobedience once your obedience has been confirmed.
> 2 Corinthians 10: 3-6

What's our weapon of mass destruction? Our minds.

How do we weaponize ourselves?

We take every thought captive to the obedience of Christ.

And **MAKE THE ENEMY PAY.**

How do we make him pay?

We punish disobedient thoughts.

How do we "punish disobedient thoughts"?

Easy:

The Greek word for "punish" used in that scripture is *ekdikeo*. It is translated, "revenge." It means to vindicate one's right or to do justice.

What is justice to the Lord?

To make His creation WHOLE again. Just. Righteous. Made complete. As in a court of law, justice is found in the judgment of the court- it is meant to set things right, to restore them to their original state before the transgression was committed.

But unlike our earthly judges, who judge according to laws created on the earth, God judges according to laws created in eternity, and the standard was set at the foundation of the earth. Follow me for a moment:

An earthly judge looks to the laws of the land it rules in to determine what is just, and what "wholeness" looks like. The earth is only one-third of a whole unit (the three realms). And any particular court is subject to the laws of the county, state, and country it dwells in, making any ruling less than one-third of a whole. This means any earthly judge can only render wholeness, "justice", to LESS THAN one-third extent. For example:

One person rapes another person. According to the laws of the land of that particular court, a judgment is made, perhaps in the form of imprisonment for the assailant, and maybe restitution to the victim or family of the victim.

Is that "wholeness"? No. Of course not. The victim still must walk through healing and restoration apart from that judgment, in the first, second, and hopefully the third realms. And now the assailant is not only bound by evil thoughts and deeds, but also prison walls: fully captive and not free or whole at all. No one won. Wholeness was meant for all. God is no respecter of man.

Nothing was actually restored- it was only contained: a fraction of one-third whole.

Of course, I am not saying that rapists shouldn't go to prison. I'm saying the earthly system does not bring true justice or wholeness. It is impossible for it to do so, in the same way it would be impossible for me to give you a whole cake that I only possess one slice of.

> *True wholeness is found in creation's reconciliation back to the original state of creation. Back to the garden, where man and woman walked in freedom and power with God, creating fruit, multiplying their gifts, filling the earth with their fruit, and subduing the land. To the glory of God. Before sin.*

This means to "revenge" the thoughts that are disobedient to the knowledge of God in Christ (who is our reconciler), we return to Adam and take dominion over the earth. We bless our earthly "enemies" (don't forget we are all someone's enemy in their minds!) and speak life to the seed and soil in that person's heart (mind). We pray for those who've harmed us and lift them up to the third realm of the Lord. We ask Him to work in them to make them whole in Christ, redeeming what the enemy stole from each of us through the second realm, and we wait expectantly to see the fruit of our good labors in the first realm. And finally, we pray for ourselves and our own hearts and mind, shutting out every thought in ourselves that tries to murder our own or another's spirit, soul, and body. In this way, we have clean hands and a pure heart, and God can do mighty works through us, keeping us safe and hidden in His wings: No harm can come to us there.

"If anyone says, 'I love God', yet hates his brother, he is a liar. For the person who does not love his brother he has seen cannot love the God he has not seen."
1 John 4:20

Get clean, stay clean.

This is hard to do-I'll admit. And the more deadly the attack against us or our loved one, the harder it is to reach this place in our souls in our own strength...almost impossible, actually. But if we can get to our souls in that second realm where the strongholds are built for self-preservation, and grab every one of the thoughts that are set to murder another or ourselves, then we can surrender them all to the third realm where Christ says, "Come to me all who are weary and heavy-burdened, and I will give you rest for your souls." I know. I'm doing it now. It's peaceful in the third realm. It's grueling in the second realm. It's impossible in the first realm.

Get clean, stay clean.

This is what Paul meant in Philippians when he said, "Work out your salvation with fear and trembling, for it is God who is working in you, enabling you both to desire and to work out His good purpose...so that you may be blameless and pure, children of God who are faultless in a crooked and perverse generation, among whom you shine like stars in the world." (Philippians 2: 12-15)

Get clean, stay clean.

In case this point is needed, I will note: blessing someone and praying for them is not the same as staying connected to them. You can do one without the other- Jesus Himself did that many times. He didn't hang out with the Pharisees, but said "forgive them, Father, they don't know what they are doing." He also told the disciples that if anyone didn't welcome the truth they carried, they needed to get outta there immediately. He actually said, "shake the dust off your feet". We can do that, too: "hightail it out", as we say in Texas.

And keep in mind, that means others can do that to us as well- it's shocking to imagine, but we are sometimes the problem. I think I was in my late 30's before I realized that some people just didn't like me. Haha! Give them grace and mercy to flow without you. Bless them and do not curse. God is for us all. And He is the one to sort us out, each one on his own. Humility is the key to abundant grace. I heard God say to me once, as a friend and I were falling out, "It's ok. You can be friends in Heaven." I appreciated that, because I knew it meant God was for us both and would bless us each as we sorted through our own issues on the earth, separately.

Get clean, stay clean.

Mankind, He has told you what is good
and what it is the Lord requires of you:
to act justly,

to love faithfulness,
and to walk humbly with your God.
Micah 6:8

Aaron and I were recently talking about a component of this war for freedom that we've been fighting. He said, for years this particular situation used to make him angry; Every time the problem flared up, he would get mad and start swinging, or collapse in defeat. But he said something happened in him last year: where there used to be anger, now has changed.

He said, *"Now: I want REVENGE."*

He's doing that by strengthening his mind and faith, by educating himself in a specific area for the solution, and by keeping a laser focus on the great vision: He's taking the land back from the enemy.

In fact, as we have walked through this process these past several years, we both can see how strategic the enemy has been to make sure we weren't aware of our birthright as heirs of the King. But now we know.

And we're taking it back.

Aaron and I are building a reputation in hell- the enemy can't have his way with us anymore. It's over, and we are setting captives free as we take back the land.

I hope you are one of them that we help set free.

We're going back into that Stolen Kingdom.

And we're taking it by force.

Journal entry:
Stolen Kingdom by Aaron Lehmann, 2018
Give me peace deep inside
That can take me to the end.
The place where nothing's left is the place to start again.
Dream it up. Dream it up. New ideas come to life.
Let dreams find their birth, allow thoughts to incite.

79

Give me joy uncontained- I can feel it in my chest.
The days that lie ahead are the ones that are the best.
Hope exists for a time- it's absurd to even try.
But the start of each new day happens in the dark of night.

So I'm coming back in that Stolen Kingdom.

Give me love, burning love consuming all of me.
Whatever's cold inside, let it feel the third degree.
Take it back, take it back to the feelings like a child.
Where doubt was not the goal, sarcasm not the prize.

So I'm coming back in that Stolen Kingdom.
I'm coming in tonight, yeah.

How much can someone take?
How much can be endured remains unknown until the trial is labored.
And the skin clings to the bone and the soul is stretched to its end.
From the Creator comes creation, all things are made new.
Pain is forgotten and life is in a new hue.
The mind ponders it all and laughter is found again.

So I'm coming back in that Stolen Kingdom.

9

The Violent Take It by Force

"Quantum Entanglement"

You abide in me. I abide in you.
We abide together: as one, alternating currents of love.

I magine with me a scenario:

You were attacked- blindsided, even. It felt like a deadly blow, but you somehow remained alive. You decided you were going to summon the courage to fight. You've armed for a fight, gathered your military backup, and entered the battleground. With God's wisdom, knowledge, and understanding, His mighty arm of power, and your faith, you took out the enemy.

As you stand on the soil of the ground you've just gained, you realize: the nurse is gone, the slave woman is gone, but that disgusting shriveled-up version of a newborn child is still in the crib, crying, and struggling to live. It's still THERE!

Part of you is annoyed that it is still there, and another part of you is suddenly gripped with fear with a thought: What if you didn't actually win? What if the mother just pretended to leave so that you would back off for a moment? What if the child grows into adulthood of all that it intended to become: cancer, addiction, disease, divorce, depravity of mind and body, brokenness, illness, financial poverty, abandonment, aloneness, homelessness, every unimaginable outcome that brings you to your knees?

And then you think: If I cast out the slave woman and the nurse, how in the world is the child still here?! Did I not command hard enough or pray long enough? Did I not have enough power? Faith? Commitment?

Immediately, the thoughts attach to emotions, and emotions turn to words: "It didn't work. It's still alive. I'll never get rid of it. I need more help. I need someone more powerful. I can't go on like this. I'd rather die. I give up."

And like perfect little soldiers, with the creative power we have as an image-bearer of God, your words take action and perform your commands.

*Jesus said: "For the mouth speaks from the overflow of the heart. A good man produces good things from his storeroom of good, and an evil man produces evil things from his storeroom of evil. I tell you that on the day of judgment people will have to account for every careless word they speak. **For by your words you will be acquitted, and by your***

words you will be condemned.
Matthew 12: 34-37

As you waver, your thoughts and fears feed the child. The child gets stronger. It seems livelier than before. In fact, it seems to be "back with a vengeance." And the more power it gains, the more power you feed it with your words, "They were right- it's no use." "It's genetic." "It's a family curse." "I can't help it." "There's nothing more anyone can do." "It is what it is."

And to the grave, it takes you- your desires, your dreams, your hopes, and your future...your very life: death is at your door. And it's just as you imagined. You feel a fool for even believing you could be set free from that child and its harassing mother. And speaking of the slave woman, there she is, with the nurse beside her, ready to pronounce you D.O.A....Just as you suspected. The very outcome everyone prognosticated. Exactly as the fearmongers believed. How could you even expect any different, stupid? Who do you think you are?

> *In this place, I want to tell you:*
> *You won the battle. Now it's time to end the war.*
> *Kill the squatters.*

Who are the squatters?

They are those thoughts that built the strongholds originally. The squatters are the paradigms that were created by nurture or nature (we brought them in and nurtured them, or we grew up with them) that set us up to fail, again and again.

They are the only thing feeding the child anymore.

They are keeping it alive.

They are like parasites- they suck the life out of their host, and then move on to torment another. These thoughts are NOT your friends, nor do they serve you well. Demolish them. When the squatters are cleared out, there is literally nothing caring for the child anymore. It will die forever.

Look:

"It didn't work" is just as powerful a command as "It WILL work."

"It's killing me" has as much strength as "I will live and declare the mighty works of the Lord."

"Hope for the best but prepare for the worst" is an oral proclamation that there is nothing stronger than the thing you are facing, and it is the power that decides what will happen.

"I'm trying as hard as I can" and "I WILL win" emote exact vibrations that harmonize on two vastly different frequencies with equally distinctive outcomes.

Here's the scientific reason why, the quantum superposition of your self-directed fate:

We think a thought in our minds. If we hold it long enough, with focus, we will attach an emotion from the heart to the thought in our mind. Once the emotion and thought are intertwined, it becomes a vibration and attaches itself to the matching frequency. (As a man THINKS in his HEART, so he is.) Thoughts of fear, lack, hatred, greed, jealousy, malice, death, evil all travel on low-level frequencies with other thoughts of the same. The longer a person thinks a thought on this frequency, the more familiar they become with its feelings and construction. They begin to get comfortable and "dwell" here. Unfortunately, according to the natural laws of vibration and creation, everything on this frequency has a prescribed outcome of death. It is inevitable. That's all that exists on that station.

> "The mind- set of the flesh is death, but the mind-set of the Spirit is life
> and peace."
> Romans 8:6

However, the same goes for the alternative:

We think a thought in our minds. If we hold it long enough, with focus, we will attach an emotion from the heart to the thought in our mind. Once the emotion and thought are intertwined, it becomes a vibration and attaches itself to the matching frequency. Thoughts of joy, love, happiness, victory, success for all, wealth, provision, health, and life all travel on high-level frequencies with other thoughts of the same. The longer a person thinks a thought on this frequency, the more familiar they become with its feelings and construction. They begin to get comfortable and "dwell" here. Fortunately, according to the natural laws of vibration and creation, everything on this frequency has a prescribed outcome of life. It is inevitable. That's all that exists on that station.

Psychologists and neuroscientists call this "heart-brain coherence". I see it as a form of quantum entanglement as well. And the Bible discusses it throughout the scriptures, in many ways, but it can be summed up this way:

> Abraham "believed in God, who gives life to the dead and calls things into existence that do not exist. He believed, **hoping against hope,** so that he became the father of many nations according to what had been spoken: So will your descendants be. He considered his own body to be already dead (since he was about 100 years old) and also considered the deadness of Sarah's womb, without weakening in the faith. **He did not waver in unbelief** at God's promise but was strengthened in his faith and gave glory to God, because he was fully convinced that what He had promised He was also able to perform. Therefore, it was credited to him for righteousness. Now it was credited to him was not written for Abraham alone, but also for us. It will be credited to us who believe in Him who raised Jesus our Lord from the dead.
> Romans 4:17-24

It's called Faith: It is the reality of what we hope for, and the proof of what we cannot see. Our ancestors won God's approval with it. If they did it, so can we. They are watching us now, cheering us on.

I can hear the stadium of witnesses roar in agreement as I write this.

Let me say it another way:

> Faith makes the thing you hope for become real, visual proof of what

you couldn't see before. Believing IS seeing.

Faith controls the superposition function.

Jesus said to Thomas, who wouldn't believe Jesus was alive until he touched Him with his own hands, "Thomas, you believe because you see. But those who believe BEFORE they see are blessed (happy)." *(John 20:29)*

Don't be like Thomas. He missed the "happy" part. That's the emotion.

Thought + emotion= manifested reality.

Faith in something, whether good or evil, causes us to attach a thought to an emotion, and ride that wave all the way to its manifested reality. Frequencies of faith are only created when a thought and emotion intertwine. If there is no emotion attached to the thought, it is just mental ascent. You see something as true, but not necessarily true for you.

Mental ascent is the culprit behind many unanswered prayers.

Here's what happens when a quantum thought and a quantum emotion intertwine. Consider it like quantum entanglement. It's the same as when our souls intertwine with Christ.

Quantum entanglement is defined as:

a phenomenon where two subatomic systems interact with each other, becoming "entangled" and remain connected forever, even when separated by vast distances.

They react together with outcomes that are uncertain until they are observed. Einstein called it "Spooky action at a distance." He saw it, knew it was happening, but never made peace with any of it because it wasn't quantifiable or predictable. But now, scientists know it is a phenomenon that actually exists in the quantum realm. Nobel Physicist Paul Dirac created an equation for it, and people call it "The most beautiful equation". And I agree: It is beautiful, even the form of the equation itself (it's on the cover of this book). But what I notice the most about quantum entanglement is how harmoniously it corroborates the understanding that once we are entangled with God, nothing can ever separate us.

For I am persuaded that not even death or life,
angels or rulers,
things present or things to come, hostile powers,
height or depth, or any other created thing
will have the power to separate us
from the love of God that is in Christ Jesus our Lord!
Romans 8:38-39

However, while nothing can separate us from the Lord once we become entangled, the connection can be disrupted.

Quantum decoherence occurs when two quantum systems become entangled, but then one system shares its connection with its outer environment. The outer environment disrupts the entanglement. There, energy dissipates, and the matter loses momentum. My brother would say, it's like being in a state of worship with the Lord, having a powerful experience, when suddenly someone turns on the lights and asks you where you want to go to lunch. Connection: dropped.

In other words: You and God had it- you were in sync, flowing together, preparing to collapse a possibility: as above, so below, quantum entangled beings. The outcome was about to manifest, but then an outside distraction caused you to take your eyes off the one you were entangled with and your united vision, losing the momentum of the connection. You stalled out because of the noise around you.

I'm thinking about the parable of the four types of soil that Jesus spoke about in Matthew 13 in the Bible. I'd like to use it to illustrate the experiences and outcomes of different types of people when they face potentially great opportunities.

A Farmer (God) scatters seed (possibilities of good things happening) and they land on four types of soil (our heart and minds).

First, some seeds land on the road (the familiar beaten paths we travel in our minds). Birds swoop down and eat the seeds up. No coherence happens at all- no one there thought or felt anything they heard- they're staying on the usual trail. Their position remained exactly where it always does… same as usual.

Next, some seeds land on rocky ground (broken hearts and minds). The person receives the great news with excitement at first, but the soil of their heart is stony, and doesn't allow the hopeful possibility to take root and grow. Pressure and hard times cause the seed to shrivel up and die before it has time to root through the rocks to get to the softer soil within. This seed and soil experienced momentary coherence, but their entanglement collapsed into doubt and fear.

Then, some seeds land on good ground, but thorns are everywhere (good intentions, but no faith in God or discipline in the heart, mind and body). The exciting possibilities take root and begin to grow, but the thorns of worry and the misuse of abundance choke out the possibilities of greatness. The plants die before the harvest can come. (I've been this one too many times to count. I have lots and lots of "I was this close…" stories.) This seed and soil experienced entanglement and coherence but allowing the outer environment into the union disconnected the flow. In my opinion, though, if the seed can make it this far into the soil of your mind, it only takes a little tuning to go deeper next time. This one is a positive move forward.

But finally, some seeds land on soil that is tilled, amended, and ready to receive great abundance prepared for it (healed, nourished, and humbled hearts and minds). The seeds go deeply into the soil, begin to germinate within the soil (heart-brain coherence; quantum entanglement), grow a root system, and a tree sprouts out of the ground, reaching to the sky, bearing fruit sometimes 30-fold, sometimes 60-fold, and sometimes even 100 fold return on the original seed! I want this one every time!

As a man THINKS (thought) in his HEART (emotion), so he is.

Proverbs 23:7 (Keri paraphrase)

Thought + emotion = BE.

Colossians 3 also speaks about the higher and lower frequencies and their fruit:

> *So, if you have been raised with the Messiah, seek what is above, where*
> *the Messiah is, seated at the right hand of God. Set your minds on what*
> *is above, not on what is on the earth. For you have died, and your life is*
> *hidden with the Messiah in God. When the Messiah, who is your life,*
> *is revealed, then you also will be revealed with Him in glory.*
> *Therefore, put to death what belongs to your worldly nature: sexual*
> *immorality, impurity, lust, evil desire, and greed, which is idolatry.*
> *Because of these, God's wrath comes on the disobedient, and you once*
> *walked in these things when you were living in them. But now you must*
> *also put away all the following: anger, wrath, malice, slander, and*
> *filthy language from your mouth. Do not lie to one another, since you*
> *have put off the old self with its practices and have put on the new self.*
> *You are being renewed in knowledge according to the image of your*
> *Creator. In Christ there is not Greek and Jew, circumcision and*
> *uncircumcision, barbarian, Scythian, slave and free; but Christ is all*
> *and in all.*
> *Therefore, God's chosen ones, holy and loved, put on heartfelt*
> *compassion, kindness, humility, gentleness, and patience, accepting one*
> *another and forgiving one another if anyone has a complaint against*
> *another. Just as the Lord has forgiven you, so you must also forgive.*
> *Above all, put on love—the perfect bond of unity.*
> *Colossians 3: 1-14*

Higher vibrating thoughts will take you all the way up into the third realm, where you are entangled with Christ, hearts and minds united together forever, full of wonder and the thrill of co-creating with God Himself.

Higher vibrating thoughts will kill the slave child for good.

Understanding the mechanics of quantum superposition, entanglement and decoherence can be a game-changer for our lives and goals if we let them.

Look at it like this:

Quantum pure state is simply the recognition of the location of a system with 100% certainty. This is the known state of being. And like the Law of Gravity, it is a lower law, like first realm existence. (Most people live here.) The state of quantum superposition, however, is more powerful. Here, subatomic (creative) matter vacillates between possibilities, an acrobat balancing on a tall, thin wall, deciding which side of the partition to jump off. It can look at the options visible and decide its fate for itself. But even quantum superposition is a lower law; it is second realm power. (Based on the Pareto principle and the law of the 4 types of soil, approximately 25% of humans live here, including those who are practicing mindfulness, positive thinking, words of faith, witchcraft, metacognition, and the like.)

The highest quantum state and most powerful law is found in quantum entanglement with God: This is the Law of the Spirit of Life in Christ. Here, you are set free from the lower laws of superposition state and pure state.

Quantum pure state is you, in the first realm, position known and identified: "reality" as you know it. It is you versus literally anything that comes your way, from either realms, first or second. In this state, you are only as strong as your latest conquest. The floor of the second realm above you can crush you at any moment.

Quantum superposition is you versus you, in the realm of infinite possibility, choosing your own fate and dealing with the consequences, for good or evil. This is second realm power. You are as strong as you have trained your mind to be in this realm, and that can be great strength. But there are even limits to this because there is another floor above you, setting your boundaries.

But quantum entanglement: now there is REAL power.

When we choose to go higher, into the Kingdom, and take our seats next to Christ, who is one with the Father and the Spirit of God, we become entangled with all that is Elohim.

We become one. And not only that, we become one with all who are entangled there also.

Quantum entanglement is you and Elohim and the angelic hosts and the myriad of the cloud of witnesses versus nothing else: if God is for you, nothing can stand against you. Here, every knee in the heavenlies and on earth are commanded by you and all those with you there to bow to the will of the Living God. On Earth as it is in Heaven. Here, we become more than conquerors. We become Kings. The earth yields to us.

Our human nature decreases and the DIVINE in us increases. Together, we flow with rivers of living water pouring out of our bellies. We no longer have to wonder where our help will come from: Help is actively IN us and flowing OUT from us, straight from the Father. As He is, so are we in this world.

The clearest earthly example of the power of quantum entanglement, in my opinion, is found in marriage. Marriage was created by God to be an earthly mimic of this power, and in many ways, yields similar fruit. The act of covenant marriage has the power to take two bodies of matter and make them one, entangled unit. "This is why a man leaves his father and mother and bonds with his wife, and they become one flesh." *(Genesis 2:24)*

For what why? For the cause of entanglement, because of the synergistic power of entanglement between two bodies, minds, will and emotions.

Marriage does what simple agreement between two people cannot do: make two become one. I tell my kids often that marriage is sacred, and sex is sacred because it is a formal and symbolic act that causes the first and second realm entanglement. And if the Lord is invited into the marriage, they become entangled with Him into the third realm. I often point out to them that there is no other person on the planet that I share my bed with, because the act of sexual intimacy is the constant unifying connector between me and Aaron. In a very physical and soulful (first and second realm) illustration, it's like a cable plugging into an outlet, transferring energy between the two systems. Unlike direct current (DC) energy that flows from one direction to a unit, (as with battery-powered units), marriage was created to transmit energy like alternating currents (AC) exchanging flow back and forth, with

God as the source of power, a separate, entangled transformer, which has the ability to modulate the two united systems to yield as little or as much energy as needed into the necessary flow. That transformer always knows which conduit needs the most flow.

But as with quantum decoherence, when we allow outside energy sources and distractions to interact with our entanglement, our energy flow gets disrupted, and the entanglement loses momentum. Energy gets dropped. Energy flows where attention goes.

I'm being reminded of the hard year (2017) when Aaron was completely depleted of hope and light, and I felt like I was having to conduct power for both of us. In my immaturity, I did it, but I didn't do it gracefully; I made it a source of bitterness for me. Two years later (and a little bit right now), I needed him to transfer the current for a time, and he did (and is), with strength and competence because we had gone into the higher realm. The Lord used that humbling time to show me that we are privileged to carry each other, power flowing back and forth, our beings conducting the healing energy of the Source of Life. And like alternating currents, The Lord God is the transformer, efficiently transmitting currents with no loss of energy. Nothing is ever wasted in and through Him. I was wrong to think that I had to carry the load alone.

Entangled in Him, we are never alone. I know better now.

Entanglement means we abide together. We remain: together, as one.

(I understand that this is not the experience of many marriages, or even constantly in one marriage. No judgment is passed, even within my own. I'm only pointing to the original intent of God's design, and to the potential of marriage to do mighty works on the earth.)

If you remain in Me and My words remain in you, ask whatever you
want and it will be done for you. My Father is glorified by this: that

you produce much fruit
and prove to be My disciples.
John 15:7

10

Faith or Faint- You Can't Do Both

"Keys"

All around me are Kingdom Keys.
I take one. He gives me three.
Again, I seek, again He sees.
And to me, He hands resources for free.

Everything He owns:
to the fullness of the Kingdom is mine.

My mom has the greatest faith of any person I know. She says it's because God was all she ever had- that He had proven Himself faithful to her throughout her life, and she always goes back to those memories when the trials come. Like David said, when facing Goliath, "God was with me when I killed the lion. God was with me when I killed the bear. And He will be with me when I kill this philistine." (*1 Samuel 17:37*)

Of course He will. He always causes us to triumph when we walk in His will.

Faith is built blindly at first- it requires trust in something/someone you haven't seen before. But once you do, and the results prove themselves, faith comes more easily. I find it helpful to create "stones of remembrance"- documented reminders of answered prayers or ways that you have witnessed God's character in creation.

I put reminders on my phone and in journals that I keep throughout the house-documented accounts of prayers answered, ideas come to life, ways that God intervened without me asking (or even knowing to ask), etc. I also like to make social media posts about the extraordinary things so that they will pop up in my timeline in the years to come. It helps to see them and be reminded of God's faithfulness. It is easy to forget even the miracles as we journey through our days on the earth- we humans have short attention spans.

"They conquered him
by the blood of the Lamb
and by the word of their testimony."
Revelation 12:11

In 2017, my husband and I were experiencing intense financial troubles. He was laid off earlier in the year, and I had closed my business at the end of the year before. Our income was cut off, and we were living on little savings. As the days, weeks, and months passed with no income, the situation became more dire. We were struggling to pay the bills and were getting further behind. Because of the earthly laws of vibration, the deeper we got, the more attuned our minds were becoming with the "stuff" on the lower-level frequencies of doom and disaster. Everything started to break in the house, we got a rat infestation, the a/c went out, my car engine blew, you know how it goes...And of course, because of those things, our relationship was tanking, the kids were exposed to attacks (the enemy binds the strong man first, and then attacks the family- this is his M.O. Watch for it!), and my body started getting sick.

But through it all, I was learning these precepts and putting them into practice. As sloppy as I was, it still worked: I was commanding life and healing to our situation. I wavered often (lots of quantum decoherence), which I believed caused the situation to take longer to heal than it should, but ultimately it worked. Close to the end of the trial, we were getting ready to lose our house. When things start to pile up, it's hard to know where to start digging. I remember saying, "when everything is an emergency, nothing is an emergency"- paying an electric bill was just as hard as paying a mortgage- we didn't have the mental clarity to make sound decisions or get creative. But God is faithful, and He knew what to do. One day, I was begging God to intervene (we never have to beg God)- I couldn't take much more of what was happening. I drove a couple of hours away, to my parents' lake house- they had just purchased it as a place for respite for our families. The house was empty, and I sat quietly with the Lord on the dock overlooking the lake.

He sat with me and began to speak. The conversation went something like this:

Me: "Lord, WHAT is the problem? I'm doing all the stuff. Have I not been good enough? Have I not served enough? Are my confessions not strong enough?" (You can already see the err of my mindset- I was trying to "earn" God's favor as I worked in the second realm.)

God: "Return to me."

Me: "Uhhh. Where'd I go? I'm right here."

God: "Do you trust me?"

Me: *thinking "no" * "Yes."

God: "Give me what you've got."

Me: "I got 80 bucks to my name."

God: "Trust me."

Me: "Ok. I'll tell Aaron when I get home."

Me: "Aaron- God says give Him our last $80. He said He will open heaven and pour out blessings on us. And mostly, He said He would rebuke the devourer that has tried to take us out.

Aaron: *with sarcasm and resignation* "He wants it? Let Him have it." (It's almost nothing anyway- we both are thinking the same thing.) *picks up phone and sends $80 online to the church we were attending in those days.

5 minutes later, the phone rings, and I answer it: "Hey-are you late on your mortgage?"

Me: *embarrassed*, "Yeah. How'd you know?" (We were keeping that one to ourselves...pride and such as.)

Family member: "Someone sent me to ask you for your account information. They said God told them to help you get your mortgage caught up and keep paying it for you until your finances stabilize."

Aaron and I: ***No words.***

A few moments after that, we grabbed the kids and testified to them what had just happened. For some reason, Aaron had the idea to call a friend who knew about mechanics. My car engine had blown, and he wanted to see if we could drop it off to have it looked at, even though we didn't have the money to pay for repairs. That friend called Aaron back, saying that our church wanted to pay for the repairs.

All of that happened within an hour of us surrendering our last $80 to the Lord.

What we later understood was that money (or lack thereof) was not our issue. Our dependence and focus on our own (in)ability to provide for ourselves, and our mindset of lack was the real issue.

The working, striving, begging, fighting, blaming, shaming, despair... each of those actions kept us in the first two realms, and mostly in the first realm.

But all it took was a mustard seed of faith, consistently watered by my words, and despite the poisonous pesticides of doubt I sprayed from time to time, to activate the promises of our Almighty One to pull us out of the pit and back on steady ground. His promises were stronger than our weaknesses and the poison in our hearts.

By the end of that season in our lives, the Lord supernaturally provided more than $24,000 to us to keep us from sinking and continued to shepherd us into the Kingdom of Heaven on Earth, full of every resource and desire we needed for life and Godliness.

I remember one day just after that year-long trial, I was still trying to manage balancing the lack, and I saw a vision of the Lord standing in front of me. His arms were stretched out, palms facing upward. On top of His palms were all the things I was constantly worried about: kids, money, house, finances, health, marriage, work, etc... He held them all, but not IN His hands. Rather, they were all floating effortlessly above His hands. It was easy for Him. And I heard Him say to me, "Take the time you need to sort yourself out. I'll hold this safely. Don't worry. I hold all time, too."

To this moment, I refer to that vision when I feel pressured to hurry up and solve a problem or move something forward. I know that as I am faithful to walk with the Lord and go where He says go and stay when He says stay, He will show me what is needed, and when. Jesus said you can know you are in the Kingdom of God (with access to all its resources) when you observe righteousness, peace, and joy in the Holy Spirit. It's not a place. It's a position. It's WITHIN us. And it's for anyone who wants it.

These are the types of "stones of remembrance" that I refer to as I navigate my journey through the valleys. Being on the mountaintop gives us a clear view of everything around us, and what a majestic view it is! But those valleys make it hard to see. Faith in God is the torch that allows the light of truth to shine.

We can have faith that the doctor's dismal prognosis is correct, or we can believe what Jesus said: "with man it's impossible. But with God, all things are possible to him." *(Matthew 19:26)*

We can have faith in our generational habits of addiction, or we can believe that who the Son sets free truly gets free. *(John 8:36)*

We can have faith in our past experiences, exalting them above the scriptures that say, "For the king's word is authoritative, and who can say to him, "What are you doing?" The one who keeps a command will not experience anything harmful, and a wise heart knows the right time and procedure." *(Ecclesiastes 8:4)*

We choose what we think about. And we choose what we bring about. We are the Kings of the earth, and when creation gets out of line with God's commands, we solve the problem.

In fact, sometimes I wake up with Holy Spirit uttering words with my mouth. As soon as I am aware, I listen to what my mouth is saying, and I write it down. Recently, my mouth was muttering:

"Solution. No: RE-solution. Resolution."

Resolution. Not solution. I heard it over and over. RE- Solution.

When we walk in the Knowledge of God, God graciously shares secrets and mysteries with us. He calls us His friends and tells us His plans. He gives us Kingdom solutions.

But RE-solution- now that's a different request. "Solution" is me to God, asking for the best idea to fix a matter. "Resolution" is God to me, telling me what is needed FROM me for victory in any battle in my life.

RE-Solution. Resolve. Unwavering determination, bringing about a predetermined solution.

Who gets to predetermine the solution?

Whomever I allow: the fake mother, the nurse, the fake child, or the Good Shepherd Himself. It's all up to me. I get to hand the keys of my life to whomever I choose, and they will drive the vehicle of my body, soul, and spirit wherever they please.

" I call heaven and earth as witnesses against you today that I have set before you life and death, blessing and curse. Choose life so that you and your descendants may live."

Deuteronomy 30:19

I know who I'm partnering with. It's a no-brainer. I am RE-Solved. I will not be moved by what I see. Then, what I believe will appear before my eyes. It's the highest law; when applied, it cannot fail.

When I've put on the full armor of God, the hits come and then they go. And there I am: Still Standing.

I've done it repeatedly and again. My Father is strong and faithful. Nothing can stand against Him.

Along with that utterance from Holy Spirit, I awoke this morning from another dream. The sum of it was the Lord showing me that this current battle will not look like the 2017 battle. It will end quickly and much more victoriously than the last because He has closed the "mechanic shops" that we used to go to for solutions, and He has made our seeds far too numerous for the "gardens" we used to sow our seed. And then, He took Aaron's legs away from him and supplied him with Holy Spirit wheels that moved Aaron quickly in the direction of the Kingdom. I broke off old paradigms and covenants I had previously made and followed Aaron into the King's estate. I saw Aaron dead in the flesh and fully alive in Christ. God used all that dream to tell me:

RE-Solution. Hold my position. Victory is here. DO. NOT. Move.

It took me about 6 minutes to interpret the dream because I've learned to recognize His voice and speak His language.

I'm sharing this to show how easily we can hear from the Lord if we just notice His presence.

God is always speaking, always with us, always wanting to co-create with us. He never withholds good from those who walk uprightly- to those who want to walk with Him.

The key is to tune in to the proper station and Do NOT touch that dial except to fine-tune the signal.

Jesus said, "My sheep hear My voice, I know them, and they follow Me. I give them eternal life, and they will never perish—ever! No one will

snatch them out of My hand. Father, who has given them to Me, is greater than all. No one is able to snatch them out of the Father's hand. The Father and I are one."
John 10:27-30

That's what Quantum Entanglement looks like.

Journal entry
WANNA STOP A WAR?
Here's what you can do:
What we see today is a manifestation of the thoughts and words we applied IN THE SPIRIT REALM yesterday and the months and years behind us.
It all happens in the spirit realm BEFORE we see it in the flesh. Even if we are unaware.
As above, so below.
In the heavenly realms first.
Then on Earth.
We do it. We make it all. God gave us the earth to produce stuff.
What we think about constantly, we bring about, by law.
That's why it's critical to know the power you hold as a co-creator with God.
Our thoughts create our words.
Our words conceive and give birth to the thing we say and inspire our actions.
Our actions, like raising a child, nurture and develop what we see and hold in the flesh- our actions grow it up and make it bigger...more of what it already was.
For better or worse.

Look:

Has the same thought in the grocery store, every time:
"I always get stuck in the slow lane."
Thinks she's gonna get stuck in the slow lane.
Looks around at each lane, deciding which looks faster.
Chooses a lane with certainty that no matter what happens,
even if it looks like it will go faster, it will stall out. Like always.
Someone in front of her needs a price check, and now her lane is slower
than the others.
If the cycle gets broken as she waits, and her lane goes remarkably fast,
she may call it "luck" but she can know that someone, somewhere, at
some time interceded for her through thought (prayer) and maybe even
through word and action.
She should Praise God for it and ride the momentum to change that old
paradigm.
Thought. Word. Action.
It's a law. It's how the world was created by God:
He thought. Then He spoke, then the thing He said came to pass
and He worked with it all.
As He is, so are we in this world.
☼*We can have God's thoughts. (You have the Mind of Christ.)*
☼*We can be His mouth. (God taught Abraham to call things that are*
not,
as though they are.)
☼*We can be His hands and feet. (Jesus said "I am the vine- you are the*
branches. Abide in me, and let my WORDS abide in you, and together
we will bear much fruit.")
☼*We have the power to bind up sickness, poverty, war, disease, and*
hatred.
God told us to do it.
☼*We have the power to loose abundance, health, peace, life, and love*
over the earth. God told US to do it.
☼ *On Earth as it ALREADY is in Heaven. He did it. Now we copy*

Him on Earth.

🔆 *God wants us to manage the earth. He has given us the keys to the earth.*

It's not: "God, WHY are there wars?"

It's God asking us: "Keri- why are there wars on Earth?

I sent you to manage the planet."

We can end war with our thoughts (prayers and meditations) and words and actions.

It starts TODAY in the spirit realm, with our thoughts of peace and love and abundance and God's good will toward ALL mankind.

Then it moves to our words that we speak- in the mirror to ourselves, to our families and friends, our peers and strangers, and to our social media audience.

And then, we act upon what we believe.

And we see and hold the things we've believed for. And we nurture them.

🔆 *Did you find even a little bit of money as you were asking God to pay a bill?*

Maybe not the full amount, but even a quarter or dollar?

That was the law in action- the thought/ desire was strong enough, and the words you spoke were powerful enough to produce a little of what you asked for.

Now, use that momentum to do it repeatedly. It clears up the paradigm you have for money, until you have the same thoughts about money as God does.

He wants you to have His mind. This is how it flows.

This is what Faith and Prayer are.

They are co-creation and military strategies.

This is how we bring FREEDOM and Peace to the world.

It starts in the mind/will/emotions. Then moves through the mouth.

And flows out of the hands and feet.

It's a perfect law. It cannot fail.

Let's take the land with it.

Test it out with something small, get momentum, then go bigger.

If we all start today, tomorrow will get brighter and brighter for everyone.

Of course, it only brings the Perfect Gift when aligned with God's WORD.

Say what HE says.

When the righteous are in power, the people rejoice.

11

Mediator. Media. Medium. Mayhem.

"What Lies Between"

The unseen and the seen,
and the space between
By wisdom was designed
to reveal the King.
The unseen makes a throne,
the seen makes a home,
and what lies between
makes a dream become known.

When I was growing up (in the late 1980's), there were 8 main channels on tv and about 30 (I'm guessing) popular channels on the radio. Cable television was just barely available, with only a few channels as well, but we didn't have it until I was a late teen. VHS was the popular mode of movie-watching, and my family spent hours each Friday evening, standing at the Blockbuster video store counter, waiting for our movie-of-choice to be returned by a previous customer so that we could check it out next. Hours.

The local, national, and global news came from newspapers and on tv for a few hours in the morning and repeated a couple of times again at night.

Cell phones weren't invented yet, and a whole family had to share the same landline phone in the house. So, if you talked to your friends, it was almost always at school or school events, practices, church, or in each other's homes. Almost everything was communicated in person, or through notes written on paper.

Music was a major influencer for teens. Starting in junior high, every teen was identified, categorized, and labeled by their choice of clothing and music: The "Punks" listened to punk rock and skater music. The "Ropers" (named after the western wear company) always, only listened to country and western music. "Jocks and Preps" were pop-music aficionados, "Thugs" were heavy-metal all the way, "New wavers" enjoyed alternative radio, and "Nerds" read books. And so on and so forth…

Each "clique" was heavily influenced by the culture of their particular sound and looked to the musicians and celebrities within that culture to dictate the flow of their identities. Same as today, of course. A little yeast leavens the whole lump.

I was drawn to the "New wave" sound: U2, 10,000 Maniacs, Tears for Fears, Edie Brickell and the New Bohemians. I loved their sound, but more so, I embraced their depth of lyrics. As a lover of Christ even back then, I was always looking for the sacred among the secular. It seemed to give life meaning, and a reason to explore. The first time I heard Edie Brickell sing, a whole new world opened to me. Her sound was unlike anything I'd heard, and I wanted to know more. The deeper I dug into the treasures of life through the songs of those musicians, the richer I felt in my relationship with the Lord and His people. I wanted to know Him more and love them better. And, I began dressing like Edie Brickell, purple suede cowboy boots and all. I was under the influence. A little yeast leavens the whole lump.

It was easy to find the Lord as I sought Him through these media: I saw His handiwork in everything-I looked for it like hidden treasure.

I remember studying song lyrics for years- I could find scriptures that spoke to the humanity found within each story and easily point it back to the Lord. Even as a "cautionary tale", the Lord spoke to me through those vibrations of sound.

A little yeast leavens the whole lump.

I also remember around that same time, dancing in the lawn of the Starplex Amphitheater, enjoying a concert, and singing along with the band, the familiar words of their hit song. In a moment, the meaning of the lyrics hit me, and I realized they were blaspheming the Lord. I knew the words, but uncharacteristically hadn't paid attention to them until that exact moment as they came out of my mouth. I stopped immediately in my track, sat down in the lawn, and waited for the concert to end so I could leave with my friend. It also moved me with sadness to think that someone could see God that way. My heart grew larger that day for those who hadn't experienced the true kindness and mercy of God, as with each of these similar experiences throughout my life.

A little yeast leavens the whole lump.

And I remember being surprised with myself, that I hadn't caught on to those lyrics sooner.

Words meant everything to me. I used to select scriptures and poems for people and write them on cards and framed pictures, giving them as personalized gifts to my family, friends, and coworkers.

A little yeast leavens the whole lump.

110

Because even then, I understood the power of words and their role as influencers: Words create worlds.

By words, the entire world was made.

A little yeast leavens the whole lump.

By faith, we understand that the universe was formed at God's command, so that what is seen was not made out of what was visible.
Hebrews 11:3

And by a word, Mary conceived the Son of God in her womb. **A little yeast leavens the whole lump.**

"May it be done to me according to your Word."
Luke 1:38

And by her words, she gave birth to the Living Word of God.

In the beginning was the Word. And the Word was with God. And the Word was God. He was with God in the beginning, and all things were created through Him...And the Word became flesh and took up residence with us. We observed His glory- the glory of the one and only Son of the Father, full of grace and truth.
John 1:1-3, 14

Through the Word, our mediator came.

For there is one God
and one mediator between God and humanity,
Christ Jesus, Himself human,
who gave Himself—a ransom for all,
a testimony at the proper time.
1 Timothy 2:5,6

And through our mediator, salvation came for us all.

"But the righteousness that comes from faith speaks like this: Do not say
in your heart, "Who will go up to heaven?" that is, to bring Christ down
or, "Who will go down into the abyss?" that is, to bring Christ up from
the dead. On the contrary, what does it say? The message is near you,
in your mouth and in your heart. This is the message of faith that we
proclaim: If you confess with your mouth, "Jesus is Lord," and believe
in your heart that God raised Him from the dead, you will be saved."
Romans 10:6-10

With our hearts we believe and are made "just"- allowed to be in the Kingdom.

With our mouths, we say, "Jesus, you're my boss- I do whatever you say. Go. Stay. Speak. Don't speak. You are my commander. I'll obey." There, we are saved- safe from disaster, disease, attacks, financial ruin, relationship ruin, fear, calamity...everything that hits us...in THIS life, and then for eternity.

Because when God sees us, He sees Jesus: the one who stands between us and God, us, and Satan, us and ourselves. He is our Mediator.

Jesus IS the God Particle.

In the beginning, we all were one: all three realms united into one tapestry, eternal.

But as above, so below: Mankind is made of three parts as well:

112

Spirit, soul, and body.

Just as the eternal realm was meant to guide the path of the created unseen and seen realms, so the human spirit was meant to guide the path of the human soul and body.

And as above, so below, just as the second realm is the womb of creation, where Jesus enters in and mediates between God and man, so the human soul is the womb of creation in a human's life. The soul is the mediator between a human's spirit and body.

A person's soul (mind, will, emotions, and personality) chooses which information gets to pass from the ether into the conscious mind, then down into the subconscious mind.

We each have invisible antennae emitting from our bodies, tuning to frequencies that harmonize with our minds, will and emotions. It is not controlled by God- it is either controlled by our own minds, or by another through abdication or brainwashing.

As information is passed to us through ambient media, we receive it with our conscious minds. If it resonates with what we already believe OR what we are seeking, we allow it to remain a moment. And if it is repeated successively, after not much time at all, it will become impressed down into the subconscious mind as truth. The subconscious mind has no ability to differentiate truth from a lie; it merely receives and believes, based on repetition and acceptance of information. Once impressed into the subconscious mind, the information becomes a ruling paradigm for the person.

Our paradigms rule our own worlds. We see this played out in each person's life. What we think about, we bring about. It's the law. How many times have you watched someone suffer needlessly over their own self-sabotaging behaviors? And how many times have you wished you could open their heads up and pour in new information that allows them to see themselves more lovingly? And how many times have you noticed those same issues about yourself? And haven't you wanted new information poured into your own brain? I remember when my husband and I were at our lowest, I told my mom I felt like mud was coursing through my veins- it didn't feel like blood; It felt like heavy, wet earth. My constant thought was that I needed a soul detox. As I am typing this now, I am seeing the metaphor: I was Adam- the man of the dust. I needed a renewed mind to understand that I was seated in the third realm, through the blood of Christ, full of life, freedom, and POWER. I got it, too- that soul detox... Ask, and you shall receive. God is faithful.

I needed better media to change my thinking.

I needed to change the station I was stuck on in my mind.

I needed a mediator.

And I got one, for sure.

Mediator
mē′dē-ā″tər

noun

- One that mediates, especially one that reconciles differences between disputants.
- A substance or structure that mediates a specific response in a bodily tissue.
- A subatomic particle that effects or conveys a force between subatomic particles.

These definitions surprise and delight me, as I have just stumbled upon them as I write this. Of course, we understand the correlation between Christ and the first definition of mediator: He is the one that reconciles us back to God. He reconciles our differences. He makes us At One with God again. Atoned.

But look at the second definition:

A substance or structure that mediates a specific response in bodily tissue.

Now watch this:

Yet He Himself bore our sicknesses,

114

and He carried our pains;

But He was pierced because of our transgressions,
crushed because of our iniquities;
punishment for our peace was on Him,
and we are healed by His wounds.
Isaiah 53:4

There are hundreds of scriptures I could use for this point-literally hundreds. Google "healing scriptures" and you will find them easily. This Isaiah one is the one that sums it up.

I especially like this next one also. It's like the benefits list in a health insurance policy, only you don't have a co-pay. The whole policy was covered by Jesus:

My soul, praise Yahweh,
and all that is within me, praise His holy name.
My soul, praise the Lord,
and do not forget all His BENEFITS:
He forgives ALL your sin;
He HEALS ALL your diseases.
He redeems your life from the Pit;
He crowns you with faithful love and compassion.
He satisfies you with goodness;
so that youth is renewed like the eagle.
Psalm 103: 1-5

As our mediator, Jesus was the substance or structure who mediated a specific response in our bodily tissue: By His mediation (the beatings- "stripes"), we are healed. Thank God. All throughout the Gospels (Matthew, Mark, Luke, and John), we see Jesus speak or lay hands on someone, and they get healed. And then the same works continue throughout the New Testament by His disciples. They do it, too. And still, in the Body of Christ today, we lay hands or speak and see people healed. You may be reading this now, thinking, "I've never seen anyone healed that way." But I have many times, and practice this with my own family and friends, and have seen amazing acts of healing. A couple of years ago, I knew an elderly woman who had total hearing loss in her right ear. I asked her if she wanted to be healed, and she agreed. I laid hands on her ear and commanded her hearing to be restored in Jesus' name, thanked God, and then left. A month later when I went to visit her, she was delighted to tell me that her hearing was restored, and her doctor confirmed it.

There is a science to it (the second realm stuff), but science was created from the third realm, and God knows how science works better than we do, since He was the designer of it. So, for the very best consistent results, take healing needs to the third realm, and let the resources flow down through the second and into the first realm. They say, "Never try to solve a problem on the same level it was created." Every problem is created in the second and first realms (the "created" realms). Solutions, like bottled spring water, are always best when they come straight from the source of life- pure, without dilution or adulteration. (I recently recommended the works of Dr. Caroline Leaf to a friend and told her Dr. Leaf could be a good source of information for her. As soon as I said it, I heard the Lord say, "RE-Source. I am the source. She Re-Sources what I give to her." Resources flow down from above, straight from the Source. Understanding this is key to humility and accuracy in solving problems.)

Trying to solve a problem from the first realm is HARD- that's where all the toil and hustle is required. In this realm, we use existing matter to create new matter, and we are modulating with the knowledge of good and evil. The Covid-19 pandemic was a great example of this. Scientists, researchers, and doctors worked tirelessly, using resources that already existed to attempt to create solutions for treatment. They were weighing benefits and contraindications, and proceeding with therapies according to results they were visibly experiencing: Budesonide, zinc, antibiotics, vaccines, Hydroxychloroquine, Ivermectin, Remdesivir, even Viagra was on the table for a moment. The problem still exists currently, but in diminished capacity. It will take a revelation from God to eradicate this virus. Thank goodness the world is filled with people who can hear God speak. I was privileged to be invited into a global mastermind group of world-class scientists, researchers, inventors, and doctors who met weekly, discussing their trials and experiences with treating the virus. (How did a cosmetic formulator get invited to help find treatments for Covid? That's another book...God is funny.) I listened as they spoke of various preexisting therapies that were yielding detectable results. They faithfully kept their hands to the plow, passionately working to end the pandemic and save lives. Many great discoveries were and still are coming through that group. I honor them for it and ask the Lord to richly bless them.

Additionally, solving a problem in the second realm allows for all sorts of junk to contaminate the solution- because that realm creates matter according to the observer, and the observer may not have great intentions, understanding, or very much faith. Instead of full healing, a person may say something like, "I can live with the depression, but I want my back pain to be healed.", making allowances for some body parts to stay unwell, but healing other parts. I've even heard people say God gave them a particular sickness to teach them to trust Him more. That idea is based on misinterpreted scripture and is an adulterated idea of the character of God. To that, I say, if my earthly father broke my legs, or poisoned me, and told me he did it to show me how trustworthy, great, and loving he was, the police would come immediately and arrest him and put him in jail. God is a better father than any earthly dad- He would NEVER do that. Another scripture people will misquote regarding sickness and healing is, "God's ways are higher than our ways". The whole scriptural context is God speaking to "sinners" and "wicked ones", not those who belong to Christ, telling THEM to seek Him, abandon their ways and change their thoughts. He then says His WORD will not return void. It WILL accomplish what He tells it to do. His thoughts and ways are higher than wicked ones.

But here's what Jesus says about those who walk with Him:

You are My friends if you do what I command you. I do not call you
slaves anymore, because a slave doesn't know what his master is doing.
I have called you friends, because I have made known to you everything
I have heard from My Father.
John 15:14-15

He tells us everything He hears from God. Everything. We have His mind.

It's critical to know what God actually says, especially since by our words, we create or destroy our own lives.

There are abundant resources available for anyone who desires to study divine healing/ divine health, and I have my preferences. It's a highly debated and sensitive topic, and without a full conversation with a person, I know how offensive healing comments can sound to someone who's suffering, so I won't go in-depth here. But I will say this:

Jesus said, "Therefore I tell you, whatever you ask for in prayer, believe
that you have received it, and it will be yours. And when you stand
praying, if you hold anything against anyone, forgive them, so that
your Father in heaven may forgive you your sins."
Mark 11:24, 25

Either Jesus meant it, or He was a liar.

In everything: we will have what we say, when we believe it- for good or evil. The law works both ways.

You can see this to be true in the negative fairly easily:

I think about people who say, "It's flu season. I get the flu every year." As soon as summer ends, they start with the confessions:

• "I need to boost my immune system- the flu is coming."

- "Better get ready- here it comes."
- "Line the kids up- they all get it, too. One after another- here we go."

And like obedient soldiers, the flu virus knocks on their front door, hands them their receipt, and hops straight onto the person...and their kids, too.

I can hear people saying, "They say that because it DOES always happen. The past is prologue."

But I ask instead: Does it always happen because it always happens, or does it always happen because it is being commanded to always happen?

(The mind set on the flesh is death, but the mind set on the Spirit is life and peace. The mind is the boss of life and death to us.)

The past is prologue when the cycle isn't broken. We fall into a pattern, hypnotic rhythm, where our bodies nonconsciously move into the spiral of the flow that we are used to. We automatically engage behaviors of habit, not questioning why we do the thing, or if it's helping at all.

Many do this in regard to health.

Many do this regarding relationships.

I've done it notoriously with my mindset toward money.

I remember asking the Lord one time, "Why is it that when you think and speak of unwanted things, they seem to manifest immediately? But for something good or wanted, it seems to take forever, if it comes at all."

He immediately put the image of a tree in my mind. I saw the big, broad trunk and its stately branches, full of foliage. And then I saw underground: its deep, intricate root system, nourishing, supporting the structure and giving it resilience. It would take a mighty storm to knock it down.

Our paradigms are exactly like that tree- the seeds of every thought produce a tree of its own kind. If our thoughts are constantly negative or "cautious" or "realistic", a tree of exact nature will take root in our minds. To ask a pecan grove where its avocado trees are would be preposterous: pecan trees make baby pecan trees, and never avocados. A consistently negative seed grows a tree with consistently negative fruit: lack, displeasure, disappointment, bitterness, despair. A consistently cautious seed makes consistently cautious fruit: hesitations to act, failure for fear of failure, missed opportunities, half-hearted efforts, half-baked results. *I felt this one as I typed. I've been here many times.*

A consistently "realistic" seed produces consistently realistic realities.

To put it bluntly: "What you already saw is what you'll always get."

That one sucks the most.

Not hot. Not cold. Just lukewarm. God spews that from His mouth.

I'm NOT having that. Ever.

Lukewarm?! "Realistic!?" No.

No.

We were created to do things no one has ever seen before. We were created to bring Glory to God through our work on this planet. Each of us. Every one of us.

"Faith is the substance (manifested matter) of things we hope for, and the REALITY of what we have NOT SEEN. Our ancestors won God's favor by it."

Hebrews 11:1

(I am running around the room, cheering, shouting and jumping up and down right now! I hope you felt that, too!)

We. Create. Reality.

We do.

A little yeast leavens the whole lump. It infiltrates the DNA and alters the substance.

Most of us have been programmed throughout our lives to think and expect the worst. The information we've taken in, the MEDIATORS that we've allowed to speak to our beings and repeated ad nauseum solidifies our paradigm, strengthening its root system. (Remember 2020?!?)

By the time we are old enough to understand that we have the power to navigate our own ships, the paradigm is already on course, full speed ahead, straight to the cliffs and over the edge.

To turn our paradigm ship around elegantly, it takes the same type of course correction as it does to turn a large vessel:

- The insight to know the ship is headed in the wrong direction.
- Knowledge of what type of ship you are steering: passenger ships take much longer to turn around than battle ships. One is built for comfort and enjoyment, the other is built for winning wars. You just here for the ride, or you ready to take the land?! If you don't like discomfort, your paradigms will definitely take longer to correct. Ask me how I know.
- A clear understanding of where you want to go.
- A precise navigation system (Holy Spirit/ Mind of Christ).
- A strong will to get there.
- Faith to know that it will all work out for your good, no matter what comes.

When we take our cares to the third realm, we entangle our minds with the mind of Christ and the will of God, and our observation of the particles become the "whatever" God promised. And like everything, the more you practice it, the more frequently you see desired results. Practice makes the uncommon, common. That's for another book, though.

But I will tell you this Covid-19 third-realm story.

In summer 2021, my cousin, Tracy became very sick with "the rona". He ended up in the emergency room, with a blood oxygen level of 78. The docs told him and his wife that if he made any improvements, he was in for a long- haul recovery. They were concerned and told them that a person in his similar condition had just died as he arrived. In fact, when he arrived, they said he had about 20 minutes before he would have suffocated to death- they put him on oxygen immediately. He told them he wanted to be home by the end of the week, but they let him know he needed to expect long-term rehabilitation in a center- that was his reality. His wife texted me to pray for him. Once he was settled in his room, I texted him, not sure if he would be able to respond. He did, and I asked him if he was willing to let me walk him through divine healing. He agreed, and we began. I started sending him

God's promises for healing, and how to stay in the "secret place" with God (the third realm). His first and consistent reply to me was, "Jesus is King. I believe it." Those words were a revelation of God to him to say- I didn't direct him to say that and was awe-struck when he did. God is faithful to speak. Over and again, for three days, he repeated that. Meanwhile, his wife was in contact with me, never repeating the doctor's bad reports (they were up and down, as covid goes), but repeated God's promises and her hope of healing for her husband. Those two strategies are KEY for remaining in the third realm. She was focused like a laser:

- Remain hidden in the secret place of God- this means you keep your mind clear of anything that tries to act bigger than God. Worry, fear, doubt, anger, wavering- each of those things will expose you to the enemy and intercept your reception. Kill the squatters.
- Watch your mouth: you will have what you say. Declare Christ's victory over every negative report and punish every thought through speaking blessings and gratitude.

By the fourth day (Thursday) in the hospital, he was healing quickly, but still with no hospital departure in sight. He messaged me two requests: he wanted his wife to be allowed in his room, and he wanted to go home by the end of the week. Staff said no way to both. That same evening, Curry Blake (my divine healing teacher) was hosting a healing session at his church in Plano, Texas. I went to the session, got my cousin on the phone, and asked Curry to pray for his two requests. He obliged, and I left. By the time I got in my car, his wife called me, screaming with joy: the hospital lifted room restrictions against guests, and she was IN the room with him!

We laughed and praised God, and I drove home.

The next morning, my cousin messaged me to say that he needed to tell me something but would share it soon. Meanwhile, his health had taken a dramatic turn for the better. By Saturday, docs were surprised and amazed that he was doing so well, and by Sunday lunch, he was home, safe, and happy. And one month later, he was performing with his band on stage.

When he got home, he called me to tell me what happened the night Curry prayed for him. He said at 3:30 am, he woke to a calm presence filling the room. He saw a figure of light on the left side of his bed. He said he knew it was Jesus, and he knew he was healed. He said he felt ready to go home at that moment, but they kept him an extra two days.

From the third realm, we all together, with the Lord spoke life into my cousin; Into the second realm, the blood of Christ mediated the particles, and Tracy's own soul agreed; Into the first realm, his body responded specifically: Healed. In Jesus' name. Jesus is King.

As above, so below.

These types of results have become increasingly common in my life as I continue to learn how to operate in the third realm. It's like learning to walk: I was weak and stumbling at first, but I am getting stronger by the day as I practice what I know. In the beginning, I got no results. Then, as I learned and practiced, I got some results, but not consistently what I was seeking. Now, I see all sorts of "manifestations" of what I seek.

A few years ago, after coming out of the bad year, we wanted a fresh start. We decided to sell our home. By the time the house sold, we still had no idea where we wanted to move and had less than a month to figure it out. I would open my laptop and search for houses online, but every time I did, I could hear God say, "You're wasting your time." I knew that meant my next home wasn't ready yet.

As we got closer to closing, our buyer asked us where we were moving. I told him we hadn't decided yet, and he offered to let us stay in our house an additional five months, as he and his family weren't quite ready to move in.

That was a good solution for each of us, so that his house wouldn't sit empty until they were ready to move in, and we could take our time looking for our next home.

Our closing day came, and we officially transferred ownership to them. Then, Aaron and I went to pick up our son at his best friend's house, whose parents were also our best friends. As we pulled up to their house, we noticed the house directly across the street from them had just been listed for rent!

We contacted the owner, secured the house immediately, and waited for them to move out- they needed another month still.

And then, three weeks later, Covid lockdowns began. Our homebuyers wanted to go forward with moving into our old house early, our new landlords moved into their new home, and we joyfully entered the new era for our family, directly across the street from some of our favorite people on the planet. Those two years in that house, at that time, were my favorite years with my family yet. It was a time of great rest and renewal for us, and it was where I discovered how to flow with the Lord. I'm forever grateful for it all.

Meanwhile, and here's a key for you:

As I was waiting for the Lord to reveal our next move, Aaron, the kids, and I made a list of what we desired in a new home. I wrote it all down and began visualizing it all in my imagination:

Dinners and parties and family events with those desired elements. I saw long walks in the neighborhood with Aaron, and cozy evenings by the fire. I heard music pouring out of every room and outside. I saw the relaunch of my skincare company and the new, beautiful branding come to life in that house. I saw my children making new friends and maturing into their callings. I saw us each enjoying our time together, creating new memories and building new paradigms. I saw us bloom.

The "where" we moved mattered not to me- I knew that God had the best place picked out for us. We only needed to decide "what" we each wanted, and to attach ourselves to the feelings those things could emote: the happiness of being together, feeling safe and loved, the joy of sharing music and sound, the fun of new experiences, and so on... but not attached to the thing itself.

And we needed to be satisfied with the thoughts of those emotions before we actually experienced them. Satisfaction BEFORE receipt is key: "Enter His gates with thanksgiving and enter His courts with praise." *(Psalm 100:4)*

Because satisfaction and joy open the gates of abundance and dissatisfaction blocks the flow. Remember when Jesus told Thomas that those who believe it before they see it are blessed? The original translation of "blessed" means "happy" *(Makarios: G3107)*. Let's say it like this: "People who believe

124

before they see are very happy." And I will say, it's not the regular type of happiness we usually experience; it comes on more as an elation, like the feeling of a great dream coming true, or seeing a miracle happen before our eyes- it's life giving-happiness. It comes on us in an instant, as soon as we choose to believe. I felt it many times during the writing of this book, as we were getting hit.

To this day, as Aaron and I walk our neighborhood or lie in bed with coffee, we speak about the future in past tense, as if it has already happened. We get the very same feelings as if it has already come, and as we speak about the things we desire to come to pass, we are actually designing their form and function for our lives and those we serve. Just as described in Proverbs 8 (go read it), with wisdom on our side, we are the architects of our lives, and God is the builder. We are co-creating together, playing with Him, rejoicing in everything He makes for us, and taking delight in His children.

Aaron has gotten teary-eyed several times as we do this because he knows: our life together used to look very different- very hard with no end in sight. But now he sees his desires come to fruition, and expansively more so now as we gain momentum. And he knows that what he knows can never be taken from him. The Kingdom is within us.

Entering those states of flow caused us to receive everything we requested regarding our new home, and more. And in hindsight, I can see that it opened us up to the deeper ways of God.

This process is necessary as part of calling things into existence that don't already exist. I call it "Sabbath Flow™." I'll explain more on this in the final chapter. It's the dessert of co-creating- delicious and so decadent.

In the future, as I continue to renew my heart and mind, and remain in the third realm, I know I will see constant, regular manifestations of the will of God and my own desires easily come to pass. I want to get results like Jesus. He said I would. And could. And should.

Now, let's look at the third definition of mediator:

A subatomic particle that effects or conveys a force between subatomic particles.

This one is interesting. The idea of "quantum superposition" is dependent upon an observer to "call the shots", so to speak. There must be an outside force that observes or chooses which direction the two subatomic particles will collapse, otherwise the particles exist in limbo with no clear direction, suspended in time: a possibility waiting to be determined.

This is where we go back again to the very beginning of creation.

"In the beginning, God created the heavens and the earth. Now the earth was formless and void, and the Spirit of God was hovering over the surface of the waters. Then God said, "Let there be light," and there was light. God saw that the light was good, and God separated the light from the darkness. God called the light "day," and He called the darkness "night." Evening came and then morning: the first day."
Genesis 1:1-5

Here we have God, Elohim, taking on the task of creating everything. He observed the formless void of Earth, imagined the possibilities, and then spoke into the second realm: "Light: Be." The waveform of the subatomic sound of the breath of God interacted with every particle possibility, commanding the future, instructing WHAT to be. And it was so. And it was Good.

And when He did, subatomic particles jumped to attention to perform His Word. It was so. And it was good.

The Word Made Flesh, Jesus is the God Particle. He interacts with the quanta, calling things into existence that do not exist.

And now, we act just like Him, sitting next to Him in the third realm, hearing, sensing, knowing the will of the Father. And then we gaze into the protoplasmic sea of the second realm, observing the quantum matter, and commanding what WILL BE. We speak. And we see. And it is good.

12

Fight To Kill or Fight To Win

"Fight For Love"

Every arrow, every sword.
Every bullet, every word.
Every weapon aimed at me:
deflected by love,
returned safely.
You are safe with me.

From as far back as I can remember, my youngest son has always loved acting out characters from movies or musicians from bands. So inspired by the talent of Roland Orzabel from Tears for Fears, he started learning to play the bass guitar last year, and went so deeply all-in that within four months, he was being hired to play live events. He moved on to John Lennon from the Beatles, learned all their songs (and picked up the electric guitar), and is now currently plowing through Billy Idol.

Last week, he asked me to watch the Rambo series with him. By the second movie, he was tying a red band around his head and walking around with a ripped shroud belted at the waist. And now, we have moved on to Rocky. We're in the process of acquiring weights and workout equipment….

As I woke up this morning, my mouth was doing that thing I mentioned earlier, where it's moving and speaking before I wake up. Then, my mind has to catch up with what my mouth is saying. I always write it down because it's always important. God is good to speak for us, and to us and through us.

Here's what I heard coming out of my mouth:

"Fight to kill or fight to win? Rambo fought to kill. Rocky fought to win. Know the difference."

At the same time, Aaron, whom I coincidentally nicknamed "Rocky" last fall because of some goals he set for himself, was passing through the room. I called out to him and told him the second thing my mouth was uttering upon awakening: "Rocky won his fights because he took or blocked every hit and kept standing. He wasn't the best fighter. He just had the most endurance."

Then I picked up my laptop and wrote what you are reading now:

Fight to kill or fight to win.

We can fight to kill or we can fight to win.

When we fight to kill, it looks like this:

We are operating in the first realm: we take from the tree of the knowledge of good and evil. We weigh everything in the scales of the laws of the first realm, and enact justice accordingly: life and death, blessings and curses. With skill, we may be able to have victory over our earthly enemies, but it will be filled with toil and terror: an eye for an eye; a tooth for a tooth. Our desire may be to put evil to rest because we hate what mankind can do to one another. But because we are trained to fight in the first realm only, we will only be able to access the laws of that realm: an eye for an eye; sowing and reaping. Live by the sword, die by the sword. Justice enacted, but only to a fraction of one-third of a whole. We may fight to kill evil, but we can only kill the source of evil from the realm we have operated in: the flesh of man. Demons are above us, in the second realm- all we can do is kill each "vehicle" that demons operate in. But as we all know, if your car breaks down, you just get another one, and usually, one that is newer, bigger, and better. Demons work the same way- they just move from flesh to flesh, vehicle to vehicle. Destroying a body means nothing to them- they eat their own and take pleasure in watching their hosts die. There are plenty more to flow through.

If we go one realm higher, we would have access to demons and angels and subatomic matter. That could get us two-thirds victory over evil. But even there, we would still have to fight hard because we would be on the same level as demons, and we would need spiritual alliances. We would still be taking from the tree of the knowledge of good and evil, and acting accordingly because that realm is still part of creation. We would still be operating in our own strength, but with the power of either demons or angels (depending on who we made an alliance with), and with the power of the laws of vibration and attraction. With our discipline and focus, we could experience supernatural power to read minds, to be invisible, cast spells and curses on our enemies, to manifest favor, change rivers to blood, turn a staff into a serpent, make frogs and gnats cover the land...you get where I'm going here...

Because remember: Pharaoh's magicians were able to replicate up to four of Moses' miracles by the power of demons. But then God, from the third realm, sent Moses power from a realm they had NO access to: Moses began operating from the Kingdom of Heaven, from a position of rest. God always has the final WORD on any matter.

Second-realm power is second-rate power. It works, but not that well. Better than the first realm, but not nearly as well as the third realm.

In this way, we become men and women of war. Every victory we have will be in the flesh only. Our minds and souls will still be lost. We remain alone. In the end, no one truly wins.

And then there is fighting to win:

This is how we ascend to the higher realms:

We can fight to win and become true champions. With hearts engaged, we are given second-realm access because the heart is in the soul, which is in the second realm, and a passion for life. We are inclined to give freely to those around us, and remain humble, knowing where our strength comes from. Our humility is our strength- the Lord resists the proud but gives grace to the humble. *(James 4:6)*

Before each fight, we know to kneel with thanksgiving and declare victory in Christ over the fight. (That puts us in the care and protection of God in the third realm because Christ is the door to that realm. No one can come to the Father except through the son. (John 14:6) We know to surround ourselves with people who truly love us and the Lord. In doing so, even our enemies can find peace with us.

> When a man's ways please the Lord, He makes even his enemies to
> be at peace with him. (Proverbs 16:7).

We don't weigh good and evil, life or death. We know what our job is, and we have faith to know that we can get it done. When we are in the ring, we don't worry about our opponent. Though they verbally threaten us as we fight, we either don't respond or we reply, "NO." We know that our endurance and resolve to hold our position in Heaven will cause us to win life.

As we fight from the third realm, we must watch for complacency and comfort- those two attributes are a threat to our success. In this, we are at risk of losing our identity, focus, and desire to continue training. We can lose faith in ourselves, and our identity as kings ruling from the third realm with Christ. I've heard it said, confidence comes from keeping promises to yourself. As we commit to the calling over our lives as rulers, we commit to the training that comes with expansion and dominion. We train daily.

And if we fall, we get up again, and begin training on a different level: we learn to fight in a more disciplined manner, with strategy and a mindset shift. We go higher.

And we win, again.

As we gain victories and influence, our wins become more expansive as well- they begin impacting more people. In the third realm, wins are for everyone. Remember how the Tree of Life doesn't weigh good and evil, but rather it brings life to all who partake of it? As we win, others win, too. The fruit of our victories yield life to those who partake: our families, our friends, our city, the youth who strive to fight like us, even our opponents, and then as we go into other nations, our victories bring unity. This is how we take the land.

We fight to win. Kingdom wins- wins for all who want it. And our superpowers are humility and endurance.

By humility, we submit to the truth of WHO we are, WHOSE we are, and WHAT work we need to get done on the earth. We keep our eyes on our source of strength, Christ, and we listen to our inner voice to guide us (Holy Spirit). When others tell us what to do in a fight, we say, "I know what I'm doing", and we stay silent, focused, and wear out our enemy. Because we know our strongest weapons are humility and endurance, we use them to our advantage and don't get distracted by what others are doing.

Then Jesus replied, "I assure you: The Son is not able to do anything on His own, but only what He sees the Father doing. For whatever the

Father does, the Son also does these things in the same way."
John 5:19

We only do what we see the Father do. We only say what we hear the Father say.

And with wisdom, we know that as we fight, there will moments when the battle seems too hard or too much to bear. We may feel like we don't measure up to our Father in Heaven, that maybe He chose the wrong person to carry that work. It's easy to give up in this place.

I have been there many times. This is what my conversation with God sounds like: "I'm not enough. I don't have what it takes. I'm not as strong as you. I'm not courageous like you. I'm trying to work on my own. I'm trying to earn it for myself… It's all too hard. Because I can't win, people will laugh at me and they will laugh at you."

But these are the words of my God. His lovingkindness endures forever.

For you have need of endurance, so that when you have done the will of
God, you may receive what is promised. But my righteous one will live
by faith.
And I take no pleasure in the one who shrinks back.
But we do not belong to those who shrink back and are destroyed,
but to those who have faith and are saved.
Hebrews 10:36-39

Fight like Rambo or Fight like Rocky.

Fight to kill or fight to win? It's all on us. It's all IN us.

Journal entry
During the very last week of the bad year, I had given up. I'd made

133

it almost to the finish line, but Aaron and I had one last, demon-powered argument, and it took me out. I was done. I actually felt my spirit leave my body- I FELT it leave- it was like tingling energy passing through my body, and then my body went cold. I went to bed that night knowing that I would die soon. I had never experienced such darkness in my life: it was anesthetizing; I felt nothing.

The next morning, I woke up to one of my dear friends standing over my bed. (Rochelle, I'll never forget what you did for us this day.) She was present the night before for the trigger of the argument, and came to check on us. Aaron was sitting at his desk, head in hands, as was his usual position that year.

She said to me, "Just stay in bed- I'm going to pray through the house."

My response: nothing. I didn't care. Pray, don't pray. Burn the house down. Whatever.

I don't know how long she was there- probably a few hours- but when she finished, she came back into the room and said, "It's over." With a hug and triumphant smile,

she left.

I immediately thought, "No, it's not over. It will never be over. Also, I don't care."

I went back to sleep for the rest of the day.

But God cared.

The next morning, I woke up at dawn. Aaron was already in his usual position at the desk, face swollen, eyes dark and unapproachable.

As I sat in bed, I heard that familiar voice in my head- the Lord, giving me a command:

"Instant obedience."

I knew that meant He wanted to share something with me in His Word,

so I opened my Bible to Hebrews 11.

134

Usually inspiring, now numb to my dead heart, I read through the list of the "cloud of witnesses"- those who "By Faith" walked through the valleys of shadows of death with the Lord, and were approved by God for it.

The scriptures say, "This world was not worthy of them."

I kept reading on to Chapter 12.

As soon as I turned the page, the following words met me:

"Therefore, since we are surrounded by such a great cloud of witnesses, let us throw off everything that hinders and the sin that so easily entangles. And let us run with perseverance the race marked out for us, fixing our eyes on Jesus, the pioneer and perfecter of faith."

I could feel the Lord lifting my head- a slight sense of hope sprung up.

Could it have actually been continued perseverance that was keeping Aaron and me from experiencing God's divine plan for our lives?

Not just that we sucked or failed too much, or didn't deserve anything good?

I read on...

"For consider Him who endured such hostility from sinners against Himself, so that you won't grow weary and lose heart. In struggling against sin, you have not yet resisted to the point of shedding your blood. And you have forgotten the exhortation that addresses you as sons:

My son, do not take the Lord's discipline lightly
or faint when you are reproved by Him,
for the Lord disciplines the one He loves
and corrects every son He receives.

(COULD IT BE THAT WE JUST NEEDED DISCIPLINE TO

ENDURE THE TEST??)

Endure correction as discipline: God is dealing with you as sons. For what son is there that a father does not discipline? But if you are without discipline—which all receive—then you are illegitimate children and not sons. Furthermore, we had natural fathers discipline us, and we respected them. Shouldn't we submit even more to the Father of spirits and live? For they disciplined us for a short time based on what seemed good to them, but He does it for our benefit, so that we can share His holiness. No discipline seems enjoyable at the time, but painful. Later on, however, it yields the fruit of peace and righteousness to those who have been trained by it.
Therefore, strengthen your tired hands and weakened knees, and make straight paths for your feet, so that what is lame may not be dislocated but healed instead.
Hebrews 12: 1-12

With those words, I came alive again. It was discipline: strength training. We were being trained to endure. It wasn't punishment. Or abandonment. Or worthlessness. Or inevitable death.

We needed perseverance. Keep going. Keep pushing. Keep believing.

I sprung out of bed, knowing I needed to share that message with Aaron. As he sat at the desk, head in hands, I approached him carefully, as he had completely severed his affection for me. I asked him if I could read something to him. He nodded slightly.

I began to read the text.

As the words flowed, I noticed him sitting up a little more. Slowly, I could see his face. Halfway through the scripture, He sat up, and finally, he was nodding in agreement.

When I closed the Bible, he stood up and came to me with a timid embrace. We held each other closely, crying apologetically

136

to each other, and to God.

I said to Aaron, "We have overcome." He nodded in agreement.

At that exact moment, his phone chimed: the text we had waited six months for: He was hired. He got a job. A very good one.

What we didn't know at the time was that job would, in the next three years, change the trajectory of our lives and family legacy forever.

God is Faithful.

His word will not return void: It WILL accomplish what He said it would.

What The Lord taught us through that very difficult time was this: Difficult life experiences come in two forms, from two sources:

- *Attacks & temptations: From the enemy (slave woman), often nurtured by ourselves (nurse). Looks like mental and physical sickness, thefts, dark thoughts, infestations, destruction of property, violence around and through you, blocked provisions, fights, hateful words and deeds, victimization, etc... These need to be shut down immediately: cast them out.*
- *Tests/ Trials: From God. Looks like opportunities to give, share, trust, rest, expand, take risks, go higher, be bigger, take on more responsibility, let go, sacrifice, have hope, be humble, let it pass, let them rise.*

You can tell the tree by the fruit it bears: if the thing coming at you kills, steals or destroys another person or yourself, it's an attack or temptation. If it has the possibility to bring life to many at the harm of none, it's a test.

Hebrews 12 speaks to the testing of the Lord- the opportunities He puts in our paths to grow and expand. Think of it like a father putting his son on a tricycle, letting him get used to riding it, and then taking the training wheels off while running alongside him. That is the discipline of the Lord. Sometimes, He lets us fall. But

He always teaches us how to win the next time...if we let Him. **"No discipline seems enjoyable at the time, but painful. Later on, however, it yields the fruit of peace and righteousness to those who have been trained by it."**
(Hebrews 12: 11)

God is always looking for managers to share the responsibility of ruling His Kingdom with Him. No good property owner would hire a bad manager to care for the land. God is the same: If we say we want more of His possessions: business expansions, powerful families, fat bank accounts, leadership and influence over His people, ministries to lead, and messages to share, we must be prepared to carry the weight of it all. The only way to carry heavy things is to practice carrying heavy things. As we get used to one weight, He adds more, a little or a lot at a time, until we have reached the goal. And then, if we want more, He will add more. This is what greatness looks like: The ability to carry great weight with humility and grace. We can do it because we trained with the Lord to do it. We put in the reps. No steroids allowed: there are no shortcuts to greatness, but when we train with the Lord in the third realm, we can take quantum leaps.

When we desire more, the Lord will test the desire. He will discipline us. If we shrink back, He will pull back a bit. When we say we've had enough, He will stop. The opportunities will stop. I hate even typing that. Let's not stop. I won't stop.

"For you need endurance, so that after you have done God's will,
you may receive what was promised.
For yet in a very little while,
the Coming One will come and not delay.
But My righteous one will live by faith;
and if he draws back,
I have no pleasure in him.
But we are not those who draw back and are destroyed,

but those who have faith and obtain life.
Hebrews 10: 36-39

Attacks and temptations ARE NOT from God, and should NEVER be tolerated. This is where we behave as the Free Woman and cast that evil out! Even if it means casting out the part of ourselves that keeps letting evil in: the nurse must go. When she goes, evil can't stay.

Understanding this makes more sense to me now as I ponder the question I asked the Lord a few days after Aaron got his job and tensions began to dissipate:

As I was pondering all that happened that year, and all that I was daily at risk of losing: health, house, cars, children, husband, sanity, our very lives, yet nothing was taken from us, I asked the Lord HOW?! How were we able to overcome it all?

His answer was loud and clear:

No matter what the enemy threw at us, Satan could not overcome the WORD that I was learning and speaking constantly over our situation that entire year. I never stopped- I cast him and his tricks out, all day, every day that year. I was focused on the fight, like Rambo. And like Rambo, I defeated the enemy every time, but it was HARD. I fought to kill. There was no peace, even in the wins. I fought from the second realm. The Word was actually the only thing that was working, though. And the Blood of Jesus.

"They overcame by the Blood of the Lamb, and the Word of their
testimony."
Revelation 12:11

Now, with faith and perseverance, I fight like Rocky. I fight to win. For all. From the third realm: Me and Elohim, and all the angels and cloud of witnesses, with full power and authority to tell the earth exactly how it's going to go: On Earth as it is in Heaven.

Now, I fight like Jesus.

And another thing: The darkest hour is always just before dawn. We were two days away from breakthrough when I quit. I'm grateful that the Lord didn't give up on me. I'm so glad I didn't give up on God.

Therefore, as the Holy Spirit says:
Today, if you hear His voice,
do not harden your hearts as in the rebellion,
on the day of testing in the wilderness,
where your fathers tested Me, tried Me,
and saw My works for 40 years.
Therefore I was provoked with that generation
and said, "They always go astray in their hearts,
and they have not known My ways."
So I swore in My anger,
"They will not enter My rest."

Hebrews 3: 7-11

13

A Time for Everything Under Heaven

"Get Up, My Love"

The seeds were planted.
The battle was won.
The crops are abundant;
Our season has come.
We must gather now.
In joy, we go.

T he instruction to write this book came as an unsuspecting precursor to a war that was looming for my family. Shortly after I started writing, the fight began, and the Lord has been using this book to remind me how to have victory over what we are facing. We have overcome before, but this battle was more complex than anything we'd fought in the past. The Lord has caused us to be two steps ahead of each blow, and thank God, I've been obedient to write as He speaks. We have won each battle because of it. The war will be over soon- I can see victory in the horizon.

But since we are in "active duty" currently, all this talk of war and fighting tends to make me melancholy- I mean, is this it? Fighting for daily joy and life? Fighting for our position on the planet. And once we win, we have to do it all over again? Was King Solomon correct when he said, "everything is meaningless, vanity and chasing the wind?" Some moments hit so hard that memories of "peacetime" can seem like a lifetime ago. I'm hearing the scripture that says, *"It was like a dream when the Lord restored our fortunes of Zion- our mouths filled with laughter, and our tongues shouted for joy! Do it again, Lord."* (Keri paraphrase, Psalm 126: a Song of Ascent)

My heart was heavy this morning- my mind was stuck on thoughts that lie about God's power. So, Aaron got me out of bed and drew me into "Sabbath Flow™": what I call the state of being that mentally positions us into the Kingdom. We grabbed our thermal tumblers, drove to the coffee shop for a fill-up, and took a trip to Dallas to look at swim spas. They were on display at the Anatole Hotel, which also happens to be the same hotel Aaron and I spent our first night as husband and wife after our wedding almost 24 years ago. I've been to that hotel many times since our honeymoon night, and even worked at the spa there for a stint, but today was the first time my mind highlighted that honeymoon detail. God met us in the parking lot today with that detail before I even opened my car door- I remembered it as soon as we parked. Then I reminded Aaron, and he made a few private jokes. Joyfully, we strolled into the hotel, laughing, enjoying our coffee, and being filled with love and the memory of when we became one flesh.

On the way home, I asked Aaron what he thought about the duration of war. I wondered if he felt like it would never end- not the individual battles, but war, as a whole, in our personal lives.

He wisely reminded me of a powerful law operating in time and space in the first and second realms: The Law of Gestation.

The Law of Gestation states that every seed has a set incubation time before it becomes its manifested reality. And that gestation period reveals itself in the form of seasons.

Spring. Summer. Autumn. Winter.

Spring. Summer. Autumn. Winter.

Spring. Summer. Autumn. Winter.

Like clockwork, intrinsically predictable. Naturally and spiritually reliable. Summer never comes before spring. Winter never hops in front of Summer. It's never a surprise when autumn shows up.

No one has ever said, "I raised a son, and then I was pregnant with him." Nor have they noticed a fully harvestable crop in their yard before they planted a single seed.

I was soaking in the bathtub one day and heard this:

"Spring is for birth.
Summer is for war.
Autumn is for harvest.
Winter is for rest."

Everything ever created, the good and the bad, follows this same pattern.

Spring is for birth: Every created thing begins as a seed: an idea, a desire, a trigger, an actual seed for plants and animals and humans. It gets planted into the "ground", with an expectation of life.

Summer is for war: The seed must fight for its existence. If the soil is conducive to growth for that type of seed, it will begin to grow. But before it grows, it must die to self- it must change. In the changing comes the transformation into its calling. As it does, many elements will attempt to attack it and end its life. If it can endure the attacks, it will make it to the next phase.

Autumn is for harvest: The reward. The produce. The seed has become fruit, visible, tangible, and bountiful for use, enjoyment, and reproduction, good or bad.

Winter is for rest: The cold, dark silence comes. Like gathers to itself. Family to family. Earth to earth. The soil must rest and build up nourishment again. The seed must prepare to die again. This season can feel like war, because it involves death and hibernation, but it is meant for rest and renewal. It can be delicious if we allow it.

This is the lifecycle of everything created through the first and second realms, good or bad. Blessings and curses.

Understanding which season each created thing is in will help you determine your course of action in responding to it.

If the created thing is wanted and beneficial in your life, then you will nurture and nourish that seed according to the season it is in. If it's springtime, you plant the seed in good soil and surround it with everything it needs to thrive. But if you worry about it and constantly dig it up, moving it from soil to soil, it will struggle to live, and probably die.

If it's doing well, growing, and possibly showing signs of life, it will enter wartime, and will need you to fight for its existence. You protect it from critters, lawn mowers, harsh environmental conditions, and the like. You know that as it grows, certain stressors make it stronger, heartier, more developed, and able to thrive. But too much stress will take it out. So, you modulate exposure and help it to adapt and grow. You train it; discipline it.

If it makes it to harvest, you rejoice, gather the laborers who helped you help it BECOME, and you collect the harvest together. It's a celebration, but even as you celebrate, you still work because harvest is work. Sickle to crop: no time to delay, or the harvest can die or be stolen. I personally have squandered many harvests and have seen many harvests squandered due to lack of urgency and appreciation. It's similar to Esau trading his birthright for a single meal.

Finally, winter comes. Now, you retreat to your home, gathering those in intimacy with you, and you rest. This is the time of reflection and renewal. Anything that needs to die, dies. Anything that needs to expand becomes a part of the fabric of your life, enmeshed with your mind, will, emotions and paradigms. That seed is the seed that gets planted again the following spring. During this time, it's critical to remain protected and safe from the elements. Winter is for rest and renewal.

The unwanted or evil things in our lives follow the same seasonal cycles.

They are conceived in springtime. They grow in the summer, fighting for existence. If successful, their harvest comes in the fall, and those who helped it BECOME collect the harvest together. Then it retreats for rest and renewal.

This example just flashed in my mind: Let's look at the life cycle of murder.

In the Bible, we know about Cain and Abel. Cain offered the Lord some of his produce of the land. But Abel offered the first of his produce- the best of what he had. The Lord respected Abel's gift but wasn't impressed with the afterthought gift from Cain. With that, the slave woman showed up and laid down on the bed of Cain's heart; there the spring of the seed of bitterness was planted. As Cain wrestled with his thoughts against God and his brother, the nurse of his ego entered the conflict, hooking him up to diagnostics, and sharing with him all the reasons he should be angry. The summer of war was waged, and the Lord warned him: "If you do the right thing, you'll be accepted. Sin is crouching at your door. It wants to take you over, but you must master it."

The nurse brought enough nourishment and defense of bitterness in the soil of his heart for it to survive and grow, so the slave child was born, and the harvest came: Murder. A small seed of anything ALWAYS yields a crop of multiplied fruit. One kernel of corn in the ground produces an ear of corn with hundreds more kernels to consume and reproduce. Cain took his brother to the field and ended his life. And his blood cried out from the ground. Then came the winter: banished from his homeland, alone, a restless wanderer on the earth. He became fearful of being murdered by others, full of suspicion and terror. But the Lord protected him because Cain asked God for mercy. God is good. Spring began again, as it always does, and Cain started a new life in a new land.

My friend and fellow kingdom entrepreneur, Rachel Jenks and I are in a dream interpretation group on Facebook. She posted a dream recently, asking for insight. As soon as I saw it, I SAW it: the way of Cain versus the way of endurance.

Here's her dream:

> *There was a man with a sword who was offering to kill people as a service-to aid them in suicide. I had come to him for that service. One of my close friends had come with me. I got cold feet, and the man gave me a grace period to decide. I was debating back and forth, scared as to whether to go through with it and suddenly I yelled out, "I want to be a mom!" He let me go.*
>
> *A guy I sort of knew (on an acquaintance level) had also gone to see this man for his service. As I walked away, the dirt bubbled red, and I knew it was too late, but I went back anyway to try to talk to him. Instead of choosing to die, he'd had one arm removed and was proudly brandishing his own sword with the remaining arm. He was smiling at the man who had "helped him" and warned me not to come any closer.*
>
> *And then I woke up.*

The interpretation:

As we've discussed in the entirety of this book, each person has a calling and fruit to produce on the planet. And not only are we called to do the work, but to do it well- give birth to life in excellence: work, ideas, dreams come true, and actual humans if we want. In her dream, Rachel was tired from the journey, and debated whether she wanted "out" - to quit before she gave birth, so to speak. She changed her mind and decided to move forward in her calling: to birth the life inside her, whatever that was, and to do it well. Another man in the dream was faced with the similar decision, and he chose the way of Cain: He didn't want to die- he just didn't want to have to work that hard. So, he cut off his ability to work well (his one arm) and picked up a sword to harm anyone who stood in his way or tried to help him. Like

147

when Cain killed Abel, His blood was crying from the dirt. He put himself in exile, as Cain was exiled. This is what it looks like to disable ourselves with our thoughts and paradigms- we victimize ourselves and harm anyone who tries to help us become victors.

We do it to ourselves.

The journey of life is hard- especially in summer and winter time. But as a mercy and muse, spring and fall show up, filled with life and love and beauty and bounty.

The events that happen within these seasons, the people we connect with, the way it all impacts each of our lives: these are the stories that we will continue to tell our families and friends. And we will write the books and create the art and sing the songs and act out the movies, and through it all, others will be encouraged to keep moving forward, and to give it all they've got.

Because in the end, the only thing that matters is: Did I love the Lord God with my everything, and did I love my neighbor as if they were me. Everything that happens is the road to get there. These are the stories we will continue to tell in eternity.

> *"Whatever tomorrow holds, we both already know: It's gonna be a long, hot summer. So, when you're in the valley, draw a heart into the ground to let the world know you were there. If you're alive, then be alive. 'Cause it's gonna end. But you can't say when. So let me pour you a cup of something good, love."*
> *Alive, by Aaron Lehmann, 2018*

Understanding the Law of Gestation will help you keep moving forward.

But just like the Law of Lift supersedes the Law of Gravity, there is a higher law above the Law of Gestation. We can take quantum leaps into the future. I'll show you. Let's go up, up, up.

Journal entry

The devil is a liar and a counterfeiter- don't think for a moment that he can bring the thing you desire. His gifts attempt to mimic the glory of God but are always an adulterated version of the truth. Especially when it comes to identity. You can know this: you will be attacked hardest in the area of your greatest calling- your "raison d'etre"- reason to be. And he will enter in through your weakest point. Search your heart and find your "kryptonite."

Then become immune to it. Secure the breaches. Become untouchable. Jesus said, "Satan has nothing in me." He meant He didn't have any areas of weakness that Satan could enter through. As He is, so are we on this earth. We can be just like Him. He wants us to. We become untouchable by the renewing of our minds. Set your face like flint to do His will for your life.

Fight like Rocky. Fight like Jesus.

14

CIA Got Nothing on The Kingdom

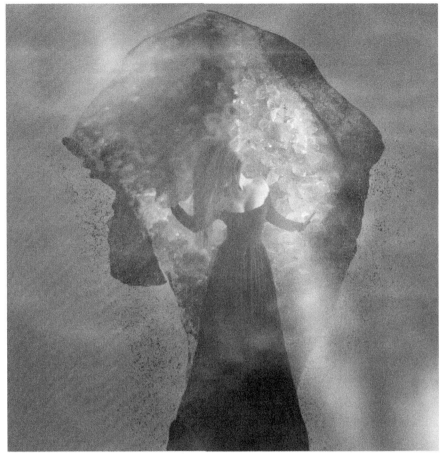

"Breakthrough"

Think it. Feel it. Speak it. Hold it.
Funnel through the Narrow Way.
Think it. Feel it. Speak it. Hold it.
Tunnel to the Portal Ray.
Think it. Feel it. Speak it. Hold it.
Welcome to your Promised day.

I was standing in the middle of a hotel room when I noticed water steadily seeping from under the wall, into our room. On the other side of the wall was the bathroom. I moved toward the door to investigate, and my son, Wilson, came out of the bathroom with a towel wrapped around his waist. I peered into the room and saw the glass shower door and its entire frame were completely removed and leaning against the bathroom sink and mirror. Water was pouring out from the shower and gushing onto the floor, and into the whole hotel room.

I yelled at Wilson. "What in the world happened in there?!?" I was thinking of the hotel bill I was about to receive. Wilson nonchalantly replied, "The frame and door came off- I was just showering."

He said it all as if it were a non-issue. Then Amelia replied, "He broke through the portal."

And then I woke up.

That was my dream this morning. I always pay attention to my dreams- I know that when our conscious mind is at rest, we are more open to hearing from the Spirit of God. I especially pay attention to the dreams that happen in the moments before my alarm goes off. It's almost always the Holy Spirit speaking to me. I always write them down.

Aaron, Amelia, and I were watching a video the night before on the CIA declassified papers on the "Gateway Process". It was a government-funded experiment led by US Army Lieutenant Colonel Wayne M. McDonnell in 1983, investigating altered states of consciousness, quantum mechanics, and psychic abilities. The papers involve experiments with hypnosis, transcendental meditation, Hemi-Synch, astral projection, remote viewing, time travel, and more. (The exhaustive papers can be found on the CIA website.) The experiments led to some fascinating theories and several techniques are still used today for reaching altered states of consciousness. I'm guessing since they knew that much back in 1983, and the papers were declassified a few years ago, they must know much more now. Of course, we know of many extremely unethical experiments performed by the CIA over the decades- I am under no illusion that they would not use this information for harm.

But as I went to bed after watching the video (I had already read the papers a few months ago), I was asking the Lord what He thought about all of it. My question was: if we are able to do those things without the knowledge of HIM, why would anyone be compelled to serve Him? Couldn't we become our own gods?

The hotel bathroom dream was His response to me.

This is how He speaks to me. And this is how He alters my consciousness: Through dreams and visions from the Kingdom.

My son, Wilson is known in our house as the "guardian priest." Jesus is the Great High Priest. Wilson had a towel wrapped around his waist, like Jesus as he washed the disciples' feet. Wilson represented Jesus.

Hotels represent public places of rest. Bathrooms represent places of cleansing and purifying. Water represents the Holy Spirit AND every resource needed for life: abundance. That hotel represented the Kingdom of God open to anyone who wants to come, and the bathroom was the Holy of Holies from the old tabernacle of the Israelites: the place where only the High Priest could enter and be in the literal presence of God.

The shower door and frame represent the heavenly (and earthly) veil in the Holy of Holies- it separated God from mankind. It was torn in half when Jesus died on the cross and finished His work: The shower door was the portal. Jesus broke the portal: He completely removed the door that separated God and man; He became the portal. And the waters burst forth in abundance, flowing without restraint into the Kingdom: Holy Spirit power and every resource needed, free for anyone who wants to immerse themselves in it.

When Amelia said, "He broke through the portal," what God was speaking to me was this:

Jesus is our High Priest who has passed through the heavenlies so that we can boldly approach the Throne of Grace to receive mercy and help in time of need. And we can do it instantly, without all the tools and tricks and years of focused concentration and applied techniques known to man. Access was no big deal at all: Jesus (Wilson) nonchalantly exited the bathroom, portal wide-open with water flooding everywhere, wrapped in a towel, ready to serve.

In the Gateway experiments, they weren't getting regular or sustained results, nor were they coming easy. They were talking hours, days, weeks, months, years, decades of sustained practice yielding 15 minutes of altered state consciousness for the most trained practitioners. And the intel from remote viewing was inaccurate.

I can get there in seconds, and get all the information God wants me to have in seconds, and come back to present state (pure state) with Kingdom solutions for what I was seeking. It took me about two earth minutes to interpret this dream, but I stayed another few minutes because God started playing a song, and doing a thing, and I wanted to see it all. Aaron walked in on me laughing hysterically in bed because of what God was showing me, and I knew he was there, but I stayed in coherence with the Lord and received valuable information and a fun time.

This is one of the things He told me while I was with Him that morning:

People can access all sorts of spiritual things in the second realm and get good or powerful fruit from it. They can also access demonic stuff, and regularly do, with bondage attached. This power can and is regularly used for evil.

But there will always come a moment when they need a miracle-something only God Himself can provide from the third realm, because only the third realm defies the natural created laws. There, the Law of the Spirit of Life in Jesus sets us all free from the consequences of the lower laws. We will always need Him. In those moments, He shows Himself strong and compassionate. There, He reveals Himself as the lover of our souls. Who could resist Him?

Then He said, loud and clear,

"Don't collect for yourselves treasures on earth, where moth and rust destroy and where thieves break in and steal. But collect for

yourselves treasures in heaven, where neither moth nor rust
destroys, and where thieves don't break in and steal. For where
your treasure is, there your heart will be also.
Matthew 6: 19-21

Our access to altered states of consciousness is meant to be used to store up treasures in heaven, not earth. The CIA wanted and used the information to attempt to access intelligence for their own purposes on earth. We are called to use our gifts and callings to advance the Kingdom of Heaven on Earth: to promote righteousness, peace, and joy in the Holy Spirit for everyone. Life for ALL.

And we can do it with ease as we enter through the open door of Jesus. It's easy, fun, and far more powerful than messing with second-realm, second-rate results.

As we do, we remain hidden in Christ, and our minds are protected from the Knowledge of Good and Evil: we only know LIFE, and perform LIFE on Earth, as it already is in Heaven.

The CIA ain't got nothing on the Kingdom.

Let's go higher: up, up, up.

15

REST

"REST"

She rested in the beauty of the wind, the sun, the moon, the stars...
In watching the trees and the fields and the forest dance...
Amongst the scent of the earth and the chatter of the creatures....
She flew with the wind and meandered with the water...
This bliss was rest...a frolic of beauty and love.
Midnight fall....let the frenzy rest on.

T his chapter is the sweet treat of this book. I wanted to lead with it, but I know that dessert comes AFTER the meal.

It is critical to know about the three realms, the two trees, and HOW to birth children (dreams, ideas, callings, and actual children) into freedom.

It's also important to know how to take dominion over our thoughts and how to call things into existence. The quality and quantity of our very lives depend on it.

Understanding the seasons, and the need for endurance allows for a more elegant transition between each turning.

But in the meantime, in the actual MEAN TIMES (they can be excruciating), there is a way to escape the terror and depression that lurks in every dark space in your mind. There is a way to not only stop your train of thoughts, but to let them pass by you, while you take another train to the third realm, and explore the Kingdom and all The Lord wants to share with you there.

Have you ever taken communion on a sailboat with Jesus? I have.

Sail away...Sail away...Sail away.

Have you danced with Him in the throne room, while the dome of heaven opened up to a panoramic view of a U2 music video? He showed me what I really needed. It was a Beautiful Day.

One morning while on a prayer call with my best friend, Amber, I could hear a train pass by in the distance. The Lord asked me if we wanted to take a train through France in the third realm. Of course, I said "yes- what do we want to talk about?" He said, "can't we just have a cup of coffee?" And so we did. And of course, that coffee led to so much more- He revealed keys to us that day on that train.

My dear friend, business partner, and artist of the works in the book, Andrea went to eternity in the shower. She asked the Lord if he would paint with her, and together, they created art in heaven. When she came back, she knew exactly how to redesign her building, and her watch revealed she had spent her total number of steps for the day- all while in the third realm.

One of the coolest stories I heard about revealing eternity on earth was, a man said that any time the demons try to taunt or harm him, he just opens up his belly, and shows them their future. Because Jesus said, "The Kingdom is within you." It doesn't go well for them.

I had to learn how to "enter into His rest" (*Hebrews 4*), because no matter how much I mastered all the things I have shared with you in this book, the time between seed and harvest, war time, continued to tear me apart. Even as I was victorious, the battle almost took me out several times.

This is my way of flowing with the Lord, co-creating from a position of REST, protected, and strengthened in the third realm.

I call it "Sabbath Flow™".

It's better than dessert: It'll make your bones fat and add length of days, years of life and peace to you.

Selah.

We're told that whatever we ask for in Jesus' name, if we believe we'll have it, then we will.

We're told that as a man thinks, so he is.

We're told that all things are possible to him who believes.

We're told that what we think about, we bring about. That we are justified or condemned by our own words.

But what do we do when we feel like we've been in alignment with all those things, and nothing is happening?

We know that the Word says, "let God be true and every man a liar."- He is faithful to keep his promises.

If there is a problem, it's always on our end: God is perfect. And He has freely given us ALL things to prosper.

We've heard that. But...

We don't know why we aren't holding the thing we believed for....

And as we are experiencing the distance, frustration...the death of a dream, the scripture resonates in our hearts: "A dream deferred makes the heart sick, but a desire fulfilled is a tree of life."

A desire fulfilled is a tree of life.

We WANT life.

It causes us to push harder, press in deeper, hold our position...any glimmer of hope inspires us to keep moving, and yet deep inside, there is a voice that nags: "It's not going to happen. Not for you, anyway. You need to quit. For real...Time to move on."

And we believe in our hearts: the voice is right. It's not for us. We've tried everything.

We feel like we're dying inside. And we don't know who to blame for the death.

When I was faced with this scenario, I gave myself two options:

Try to muster the inspiration to keep moving forward in futility (even though that had been my Modus Operandi always). Or-

Give up the dream entirely and try to forget that I've seen what was possible to him who believed...try to forget that I've seen my own future- and it was full of dreams-come-true.

Both options made me want to vomit.

So, I opened my journal and wrote this:

"I don't want to fight anymore. I don't want strife or striving. I want FLOW.
Lord, life is filled with struggles- even something as simple as exercising daily is an issue for me.
It is all hard.
Is there a place in your design for easy flow at all times?
Creative output without exhaustive input?
I don't want to fight anymore.
I'm hearing now: To live is Christ; to die is gain.
I want to live in Christ. I don't want to die without fulfilling my calling.

But I am weary.
I hear you saying, "Come unto me all who are weary, and I will
give you rest."
I receive your rest. I desire your creative flow.
I desire to create with divine design.
As Wisdom, at the side of Elohim, delighting in all you have made,
Lord.
I want FLOW.
I want to easily attract your resources. Your relationships. Your
health & healing.
Your love. Your righteousness.
I want peace and Joy in the Holy Spirit."

And with that, the Lord reminded me that there was a place of REST for those who will enter into it.

I decided I wanted it: a Sabbath rest from MY OWN works.

Suddenly, I was inspired to take action.

I did what I knew to do:

"Write down this vision;
clearly inscribe it on tablets
so one may easily read it.
For the vision is yet for the appointed time;
it testifies about the end and will not lie.
Though it delays, wait for it,
since it will certainly come and not be late.
Look, his ego is inflated;
he is without integrity.
But the righteous one will live by his faith.
Habakkuk 2:2-4

I created a great vision for my Sabbath rest- the WHY- the end place:

To create generational wealth & autonomous businesses that serve nations through application of Biblical wisdom, understanding & knowledge.

I named the rest: **FLOW;** I set my intention: **"Careful Investments,"** and then listed the goals of the process.

I put them all on a vision board, and then created a schedule of daily activities that I thought would lead me into flow. I made a list of promises from God, and then set a start date for the rest.

Then I told myself I would give myself a break from the doubts, thoughts, and worries that continued to pop up- I would deal with them after 30 days.

"Go easy on yourself," I told myself that daily, constantly.

I wrote *"Take the path of least resistance"* on my bathroom shower wall- my weakness was constant self-criticism and wavering. I knew this would ease those thoughts.

The first week of the sabbath, as I began moving on the schedule, the Lord immediately showed me a flaw in my plan:

I was still "WORKING" to solve my issues- I had a membership to a program that would help me with my desire, and I planned to run through the course over the next 30 days.

But the Lord revealed to me that unless my heart issue was healed, the course would be more work and striving, and a waste of sabbath rest. I would miss it.

I also made a schedule for all the stuff I was going to do during my "rest."

When I proudly showed my mom my schedule and vision board, she said, "That sure looks like a lot of work..."

I said, "What am I supposed to do?! Sit on the couch for a month, eating bonbons and watching tv?"

"Yes.... you could do that...or take walks or naps or bubble baths...be with your family. Cook new recipes... dance on the back porch with Aaron...enjoy the days..."

My immediate response to that kind of "laziness and lack of discipline" was to dismiss it. It would never solve my problems.

But my mom QUICKLY reminded me: what I was doing now wasn't

solving my problems either…and I was doing a LOT of work…

She suggested that I totally, completely rest from my work and problems-just for 30 days.

"Give yourself permission to rest," she said.

I'm hearing Queen Esther now: "If I perish, I perish."

Mom was right.

About three days into my "struggle into rest," I had a meltdown.

I was in the car with Aaron, sobbing and listing the litany of problems that I had YET to solve, and how useless my hands and brain were to fix my problems.

"WHAT AM I SUPPOSED TO DO?!? I'm doing all of it!"

As Aaron sat like a statue in the passenger seat, not moving an inch, I noticed a car parked in a driveway along the street.

The license plate read: "Ask FLO."

It caught my attention.

"Look, Aaron- do you see that?"

"Yes," he nodded, still frozen.

"Hmmmm…," I thought.

A few miles down the road, I saw a street sign.

"Flo Ave."

Well, look at that.

Once I got back home and went to my vision board, there it read, big and bold:

"FLOW."

In that moment, I threw away my goals and plans, kept the name FLOW.

Instead, The Lord began showing me what the real issue was: Subconsciously, I thought I had to EARN every blessing and success from God. I did all the "stuff", but it never seemed to be enough-the results never met my expectations. And my default would land on, "You still haven't worked hard enough. You weren't disciplined enough. You didn't show up enough…"

I kept hanging out in the second realm on this issue, because I knew I could manifest things if I held my confessions long enough…only, I was too exhausted to hold on any longer.

I was trying to get in harmony with the laws that govern resources on earth but was in dissonance with the laws that governed prosperity in heaven- the higher law that said that I was an HEIR to all that was His, and I had access to it all without having to bust my bum getting it all. I was the older brother in the story of the prodigal son.

Once I saw that, I relaxed, laid down the program, and began to move forward in righteousness, peace, and joy. And it worked.

The Lord called me constantly, all day, to His presence through dreams and visions. I experienced His presence in ways I'd never known before, as I took baths and naps and walks, just being still and quiet. I wrote everything down- it was all too delicious- I didn't want to forget a single thing.

Every moment of my day became a gift and a pleasure, and my attention to the irritations of life disappeared. I assume they were still happening, but I certainly didn't notice them.

When my 30-day sabbath was over, The Lord had transformed my paradigm, and introduced habits to know God's good, pleasing, and perfect will, full of rest and flow.

Resources began to open, flowing with ease as needed.

I had begun unclogging the pipeline to receiving. Finally.

And then the clarity came, causing my actions to be inspired instead of contrived.

Life became pleasurable and my work became so much fun!

Shortly after the sabbath ended, my husband and I were having a glass of wine on our back porch. I asked him, "Are you glad you married me?"

His reply was, "I have really enjoyed you these past 30 days."

I laughed because I knew it was true- we've been married for 24 years, but the highlight of our years together was when I finally learned to chill the heck out and flow with the Lord!

For that, I am grateful.

The truth is that expansion and greater expression of the Lord in our lives is not only our birthright, but it's in our very DNA.

Create or disintegrate: it's a natural law of life.

And the higher law above that says that we are set free to be, free to expand.

We choose to create or disintegrate.

We choose life or death.

We don't realize how much control we have over our lives, and because of it, we abdicate our power to our circumstances and the lower powers of this earth.

We do it.

It isn't done to us.

We have the power to give it away and we have the power to take it up again.

Just like Jesus.

As He is, so are we in this world.

The disciples returned from doing what Jesus sent them out to do (heal the sick, raise the dead, cast off demons: bring the good news to the people). They were rejoicing at how easily they were able to get their work done and were amazed that even demons obeyed them.

But look at what Jesus said to the disciples:

> *I watched Satan fall from heaven like a lightning flash. Look, I have given you the authority to trample on snakes and scorpions and over all the power of the enemy; nothing will ever harm you. However, don't rejoice that the spirits submit to you, but rejoice that your names are written in heaven."*
> *Luke 10:18-20*

Jesus wanted them to know: Satan fell, and his demons with him, to the second realm. The disciples were operating in the third realm, with ease and flow. The enemy is defeated, and we have been given power over them all. But what's most important is not the power we have over the enemy, but rather, that we sit in the third realm, in victory and rest.

Our sights aren't to be focused on the enemy and the fight. Our true nature and calling on this earth is to take dominion over the land by being fruitful, multiplying our fruit, filling the earth with the goodness of our fruit, and ruling over our territory with righteousness, peace, and joy in the Holy Spirit.

The fight is part of it.

But the fight is NOT the point.

Sabbath Flow™ is the point: We are seated with Christ in the third realm. And together, we create, on Earth as it is in Heaven.

It's so much fun for God. It should be fun for us, too.

The more we practice subduing the works of the enemy and causing creation to yield to the fruitful nature of God, the easier it flows through us.

As my husband beautifully wrote in a song,

"Living Word spoke for me. Living Word speaks to me. Living Work speak through me."

In Him, we live, move, and have our being.
In Him, we live, move, and have our being.
In Him. I live. I move. And I have my entire being.
In Christ. I Am.

(Excuse me, please. I'm having a moment. Can you feel it, too?)

Our latter days were meant to be greater than our former days as we grow and build and expand. It was part of God's original intent in the Garden, and we will experience it fully when we return to eternity. *He satisfies our desires with good things so that our youth is renewed like the eagle's. (Psalm 103)*

We can see and experience this freedom to thrive in THIS life, in THIS time, as part of the redemption of Christ, as He reconciled man back to God.

Sabbath Flow™ is the dessert of your life. Dessert is delicious and indulgent, and sweet and fun, and the Lord gives it to us in the good times as a celebration of life, and in the bad times as a refreshment during the war. Sabbath Flow™ is just like that.

Let's Flow.

The following chapter is the first chapter of my next book, "Sabbath Flow™." Digest the previous chapters of this book: they are meat and nourishment to your life as a mature son of God. As you allow the precepts to tear down old paradigms and renew your mind, put them into practice and begin to gain momentum toward your new life as ruler over the earth. Meanwhile, I'll be plodding away at finishing the next book, and you can go directly into Sabbath Flow™, creating with ease and joy, from the third realm. It will include a 30-day challenge to learn how to flow with God. Get ready: the best is yet to come.

16

Sabbath Flow™

"The Great Expanse"

It was there in the great expanse when she became aware that her power was from within... That she was one with the power, she was born of the power; She was with God. Nothing else was needed, not wind, nor color, nor title... No force but love... She was with God in the great expanse.

Τhe WAR for Fulfillment.

What if you didn't have to work so hard for success?

What if you got hold of a little bit or a whole bunch of stuff you didn't "earn", and you were grateful and used it to grow and multiply and expand GOOD on the Earth?

And what if your dedication to the multiplication and expansion of the thing didn't cost you your marriage, family, children, relationships, health, and integrity?

What if we could be TRULY HAPPY exactly where we are at, in the present moment, doing the thing that's in front of us, in full confidence that it will create MORE happiness for us and others?

What if you could say: "I am where I am, and it's good."?

Let me see if I can explain it better:

When we operate outside of the REST of Christ, we work hard, trying to crush it, slay it, earn it, hustle, and grind it... and the top 2% of those trying WILL win it.

The strongest survive.

They operate with iron will in the second realm- the created, unseen realm, where all subatomic matter exists.

Their works and confessions cause it to BE.

It works for the 2%.

And many admire and want to know HOW they did it.

So sometimes they create courses and write books to share their wisdom, which they have definitely "earned", but only a few can follow their path and yield similar results because there is a cost to that path to success that not many are willing to pay.

And I'm not talking about the "sacrifice" of pleasure for hard work- even broke people do that daily- they have to, not for "sacrifice" but rather necessity.

The cost I'm talking about is:

Marriage. Family. Health. Relationships. Integrity. Boundaries. Joy.

Hope...
Your very LIFE.

We have been taught that money is the highest form of exchange for value given to the marketplace.

And so, we judge our work- the value we bring-by the number of dollars given in exchange for our work.

When a person gets lots of dollars for a work, they deem themselves "worthy", and raise their own value, feeling accepted on some perceived higher level.

They tell everyone how valuable they must be because look how many dollars people have paid them for their work!

But then they look outward and see someone with more dollars received, more platforms of influence, and esteem that person as a more valuable person.

And the hustle gets turned UP.

They strive harder to become more valuable to the market.

Relationships, physical and emotional health suffer more, boundaries get crossed, integrity becomes blurred....

But if the person is strong enough, and has a strong will, they will hit the goal again.

And they will outwardly look accepted and successful, but inwardly, not be satisfied. They have still more to prove, more to gain.

And the poor, broke souls who are trying to emulate them lose it all, too. Because their focus never shifts away from the $$$. Even in the not having, they still lose:

Spouses, children, family, relationships, health, peace, joy.

Lost because they've seen it's possible, just NOT FOR THEM.

I've seen it repeatedly and again. I've tried it, too. I don't have the stamina to keep up though- I'll admit it.

I've sat in rooms full of extremely "successful" people, knowing bits of their personal lives, knowing the wake of destruction that followed in their path to success. I've coached some of them- I've felt the pain of their loss. I almost lost it all myself, five years ago…

I recently read a book on how to do a certain thing in a certain short amount of time and it would lead to becoming very rich.

The author also mentioned that the day that he got his first multimillion-dollar check was also the day his wife moved out. He sat in an empty house, trying to find joy in his accomplishment.

He was honest enough to admit the cost was high.

He went on to say he had to go through a time of great soul healing afterward.

But this does not have to be so.

There IS a way to walk in righteousness, peace, and joy AND have every need met, every bill paid, every resource for every good work freely given to you as needed.

And it is easy and as light as you want it to be.

There is abundance for us all, and it is right, and pure and good to want it…it's OURS, as an inheritance from a very, very rich Father. He wants us to have it.

It's found in Sabbath Rest, and looks much different than what we are taught, but the reward is FULL of life, in abundance.

When I fall back into "hustle" mode, looking at the dollar to determine the success of any work I've done or need to do, the Lord recalibrates my vision, reminding me that rich people would pay GOOD MONEY for healed marriages, healed bodies, happy families, and healed minds and emotions, if they knew they could get it. The money they busted their bums to get- they would spend it on restoring the carnage of the war to success if they thought it was possible.

He tells me to seek Righteousness, Peace, and Joy in the Holy Spirit- that's where anything and everything is added to your account.

172

Then He shows me the list that He looks at:

- How's my obedience to Him?
- How's my husband's heart- does he feel safe with me?
- How are my kids? Do they lack any good thing from me?
- How are my parents and siblings experiencing me? Am I showing them love and honor?
- How's my health? Am I taking physical care of my soul-suit?
- How's my heart? Am I bitter? Jealous? Envious? Gossiping? Creating factions? Being petty? Fearful? Doubtful? Restless? Worried? Self-absorbed?
- How are others experiencing me? Do they feel attacked or pressured by me? Am I short or impatient with them? What message am I putting out on social media? Arguing? Wanting to be right?

All of these things are vastly more important than the numbers in my bank accounts, immediately and ultimately affecting the flow of my life:

They are Life and Death to the quality and quantity of my participation on this Earth.

They control the flow of access to the Kingdom of Heaven on Earth, and all it contains.

And I keep thinking, what if it never had to go that far- if in the striving for the successful accomplishment of worthy ideals, nothing valuable took a hit: not you, not the spouse, not the kids, not family, not the mind or emotions or health...

What if the only things that died in the process are our own pride and self-will...our doubts and evil desires...our fears and ego?

And I hear the Lord say, *"Yes. That's how it should be-*
I came that you would have LIFE and have it ABUNDANTLY."
All of it.

And then I look at the setup for the Israelites in the wilderness:

Miraculously escorted OUT of slavery, never lacked water, were given magical food every single day, not a feeble one among them, feet never swollen, clothes never worn out...yet, their hearts were tested again and again... it took them 40 years to sort it out, and half of them never got to walk into the promised land because of their own mouths and confessions. God became to them AS THEY SAID.

I AM that I AM.

God gave the ones who believed and OBEYED His order to GO IN, a WHOLE KINGDOM full of crops they didn't plant and animals they didn't raise and streams and iron and copper (not including the HAUL of gold and silver freely given to them by the Egyptians when they left).

He gave them an entire land full of stuff they never earned.

All He asked from them was to do what He said, and don't grow proud, thinking they "earned" any of it. He said, "Don't forget it was I who did all of this."

God is our source of supply. Obedience and REST in Him is our key to access.

I'm living it out currently, watching how it flows as Aaron and I stay focused on our vision. As we do, we are keenly aware of the flow as we switch from trusting the process to falling into fear and doubt, and I will say: things shut down FAST when the doubt and fear comes.

When you don't know what you are going to eat, where you will sleep,
what clothes you will wear, and are STILL joyful,
You are THERE.
That's The Kingdom of God, where access to EVERY resource exists.
It's there that you get in the river and FLOW.

We know now that the place where all the "stuff" we need and want is in the Kingdom of God- that third realm, and the "door", the portal to go inside that realm is Jesus. We know that the "stuff" are seeds that get dropped into the womb of creation- the second realm and gestate according to how well they are nourished in the womb by our confessions, thoughts, and the grace and mercy of the Lord. We know that the "stuff" is born into the world in the first realm, the manifestation of what we willed to life.

The function of Sabbath Flow™ is to create space in your mind for the good that you desire. Tension, fear, doubt, thoughts of lack and limitation- they each create resistance in your mind, and in the vibrational fields of energy. In short: they block the flow of receiving. As Jesus said, "Fear not: only believe."

As we believe that God is who He says He is, and He WILL do what He says He will do, and we allow ourselves to become entangled with Him, alternating currents of energy, we will see the flow:

His strength and grace modulating in you; Your desires and creative ideas flowing back to Him, delighting and inspiring Him to do the thing you desire: Co-creating on Earth as it already is in Heaven. As above, so below. This is Sabbath Flow™.

Follow me...I'll take you to the river.

__Journal entry (Written in 2021, During my 30-day Sabbath Flow)__
War is hard. And tolling.
But as a mercy, is often met with bouts of amusement and release.
Today was no different.
During my rest today, I asked the Lord to share something with me that
He wanted me to know or experience with Him.

I immediately saw Jesus as I did in a dream, back in 1994:
My husband, Aaron (my then boyfriend) and I had just broken up and
my heart was aching. I was inconsolable for weeks.
One morning, the Lord came to me in a dream.
I was sitting in a high school field with several teens, and we were all
mourning the death of a friend. As we were crying, the sun was eclipsed
by the form of a person standing over me. I looked up at the figure but
couldn't make out the details because of the shadow. I could only see his
eyes: piercingly clear, and I could see into his soul.
It was Jesus.
He was surrounded by love and light.
He extended His hand to me and lifted me up from the ground.
He pulled me into Him and held me tightly, full of warmth and security.
I knew I was going to be ok.
I woke up that morning feeling loved, surrounded, and whole.
He healed my heart that day.

Back to today: that same vision came to mind-
Jesus, eclipsing the sun, standing over me, lifting me up and pulling me
up to Him.
Only this time, we began to dance.
First, we were back on that high school field-
I was in a red dress and he was in a military uniform.
As he twirled me around, I could hear the song,
"Lady in Red" (Chris de Burgh Song, 1986) playing in the background.

As the song ended, I expected Him to twirl me back around and hand
me to Aaron,
but He didn't.
Instead, we were in the throne room, standing in front of God the
Father,
and the ceiling opened up to the sky.
The song, "Beautiful Day" (U2, 2000) started to play,

and Jesus said, "Let's keep dancing! And LOOK!"
We ended up completely outside, dancing, jumping, and going in circles,
as the lyrics of the song played out like a movie across the sky, all
around us:
I saw every detail described in the song, a panoramic display of the
beauty of all creation, and God's delight in the sons of man.

When it was over, I knew:
Everything I'll ever want, anything I'll ever need
will come in due time.
I only need to remain with Him. At rest and play.
Enjoying the beautiful days.

Afterword

Take the Land.

I began writing this book in November 2022. I was in the sauna, getting into flow, and the Lord interrupted my train of thought with a strong command:

"Write about the slave woman dream."

I have been working on a book about the laws that govern the two lower realms for about a year; it seemed to be a distraction to begin another book while still working on that one. But the command was clear and strong.

I began writing in that instant. I had no vision for this book- I didn't even know where I was going with it. I just wrote what I was hearing as I typed.

As I did, every word flowed effortlessly. Each day as I wrote, when the words stopped, I stopped. That helped me only say what I heard the father say. No more, no less.

A couple of weeks after I started writing, my family entered a season of war, attacked at once in every area a person can fight: relationships, health, and finances. This book became the War Plan for our military campaign. The Lord was always revealing truth a day or two ahead of each attack, and He navigated me through each battle with the writings from the days before. We have won every battle because of it.

One day during this time, halfway through the day, a seed of thought was planted in my mind- not by God (that's all that matters). I took that seed and gave it to the "nurse." She planted it, watered it, nurtured it with fear, anger, and pride, and brought the sprouted plant home to my family. Even as I was preparing to fight, through tears of rage, I told my husband I could hear the Lord saying, "A wise woman builds her house, but a foolish woman tears it apart with her own hands." Aaron said, "Well just stop." But I was holding the manifested "slave child" plant, the sapling from tree of the Knowledge of Good and Evil, and my train of thought was moving full speed ahead. Aaron even said, "I can see that nothing can stop you with this." We each ate its leaves, and bitterness was its flavor. Within two minutes of conflict, the whole household was engaged, and destruction was imminent. I immediately saw my error and began the de-escalation. "Wait a minute! Wait a minute! Wait a minute!" Those words were my white flag. I was wishing that I had followed the war plan- the Lord was telling me, as I was preparing to fight my family that night, "Kill the squatters. Kill the squatters. Kill the squatters. THEY (my family) aren't the squatters!" I refused. The nurse wanted results in the first realm, not the third realm, and she wanted them NOW. As I write this now, I am hearing words from a song Aaron wrote about our marriage:

> *"She's the only one with my heart in her hands. With a word, she can raise or crush this man. And she does. Sometimes, she don't know, don't know what she's doing. She's perfect for me, but she's only human."*
> *Perfect, by Aaron Lehmann, 2018*

Because we've built a foundation of love and trust in our family, I was able to pull back and apologize, and by the end of the evening, everyone was at peace again, mostly. If we hadn't, my ship would have sunk that night. I blew it. Big time. But as Bono says,

> *"Only love can heal such a scar."*

But if it were 2017, it would have taken much more for us all to heal. I'm grateful to be past those days and those paradigms. As we as a family have continued to walk with the Lord and learn His ways, we have been able to elevate our minds and emotions, steadily creating a trail of success behind us for others to walk in.

As the Psalm says, "surely goodness and mercy will follow me all the days of my life…"

As I end this writing, I want to leave you with this:

> *So then, my dear friends,* **work out your own salvation with fear and trembling. For it is God who is working in you, enabling you both to desire and to work out His good purpose.** *Do everything without grumbling and arguing, so that you may be blameless and pure, children of God who are faultless in a crooked and perverted generation,*

among whom you shine like stars in the world.
Philippians 2:12-15

I now know the vision for this book: to be a light that exposes the true impotence of darkness, to share the War Plan for birthing and raising free children into freedom, and to guide my family through a very specific engagement with the enemies of our freedom. This time, we fought safely from the third realm, as true sons and daughters of the King.

We have taken our seats on our thrones.

Now: we take the land.

About the Artist

photo credit: Keri Lehmann

Andrea Calvery is an award-winning master photographer, entrepreneur, artist and speaker. Andrea is the founder of Atelier Antiques and Transcend Fine Art Gallery in Historic Downtown Waxahachie, Texas. Andrea is an alchemist of visionary storytelling and brings honor to lives through creating one-of-a-kind conceptual art from this beautiful journey we call life. Her motto: "Art is love, love is art, and all that lies between."

For more ways to interact with Andrea, find her at the following online platforms:

Website: https://www.andreacalvery.com/
Facebook: @andreacalveryphotographer
Instagram: @andreacalveryportrait
email: andreacalvery@gmail.com

About the Author

photo credit: Andrea Calvery

Keri Lehmann is an entrepreneur, vision builder, natural cosmetics formulator, speaker and writer. She is the founder of Savvy Bohème Preeminent Skincare, Made To Become Vision-Building Workshops, and Flow: The Two-Hour Retreat. Fueled by three passions: Kingdom + Vision + Beauty, Keri plays to her strengths to create products and services that bring value to those she is called to serve.

Keri lives in Texas with her husband, Aaron, her children, a fat dog and cat, and all her family and friends. She always says, "I've had the same loves my whole life: God, family, friends, Aaron Lehmann, and U2." This statement remains true.

For more ways to interact with Keri, find her at the following online platforms:

Website: https://www.kerilehmann.com
   Facebook: https://www.facebook.com/flowwithkeri
   email: keri@kerilehmann.com
   Private Facebook Group: https://www.facebook.com/groups/savvyhang out

And for Vision Coaching, check out Keri's online or in-person workshop, *Made to Become.*
   It's a powerful, FAST, and effective approach to discovering your divine calling in life.

Made in the USA
Middletown, DE
25 April 2023

29224592R00119